Stars of Wisdom

Stars of Wisdom

Analytical Meditation, Songs of Yogic Joy, and Prayers of Aspiration

KHENPO TSÜLTRIM GYAMTSO

Foreword by the Fourteenth Dalai Lama
Foreword by the Seventeenth Gyalwang Karmapa

Translated, Edited, and Introduced by
Ari Goldfield and Rose Taylor

 SHAMBHALA · *Boston & London* · 2010

Shambhala Publications, Inc.
Horticultural Hall
300 Massachusetts Avenue
Boston, Massachusetts 02115
www.shambhala.com

9   8   7   6   5   4   3   2   1

First edition
Printed in Canada

♾ This edition is printed on acid-free paper that meets
the American National Standards Institute Z39.48 Standard.
♻ This book was printed on 100% postconsumer recycled paper.
For more information please visit www.shambhala.com.
Distributed in the United States by Random House, Inc.,
and in Canada by Random House of Canada Ltd

Designed by James D. Skatges

Library of Congress Cataloging-in-Publication Data
Khenpo Tsultrim Gyamtso, Rinpoche, 1934–
Stars of wisdom: analytical meditation, songs of yogic joy, and prayers of aspiration /
Khenpo Tsultrim Gyamtso; foreword by the Fourteenth Dalai Lama; foreword by the
Seventeenth Gyalwang Karmapa; translated, edited, and introduced by Ari Goldfield and
Rose Taylor.—1st ed.
p.   cm.
Includes index.
ISBN 978-1-59030-775-5 (pbk.: alk. paper)
1. Spiritual life—Buddhism. I. Goldfield, Ari, 1969– II. Taylor, Rose, 1970– III. Title.
BQ5675.K48 2010
294.3′442—dc22
                                          2009034483

In the publication of this book, special thanks go to all of the sponsors of the Marpa Foundation. It is because of their generosity that we are able to publish this book of Khenpo Tsültrim Gyamtso Rinpoche's wonderful teachings, and we are very grateful to them.

Contents

PART THREE

Mahayana Aspiration Prayers

THE DALAI LAMA

Foreword

WE TIBETANS HAVE been custodians of the full range of the Buddha's teachings for well over a thousand years. These have been analyzed, refined, and most important of all put into practice, becoming the mainstay of Tibetan culture. Indeed, the principles of compassion and nonviolence are among the distinguishing marks of the Tibetan way of life even today.

Until 1959, many conditions contributed to the flourishing of Buddhism in Tibet. However, what gave it vigor was that down the centuries individuals continued not only to read, memorize, study, and debate, but also to retire to caves and other remote locations to meditate, just as great luminaries of the past, like Milarepa, had done. In the upheavals that followed 1959 the freedom to do this in Tibet has been severely constrained.

Khenpo Tsültrim Gyamtso Rinpoche is one of a steadily dwindling number of those who undertook their study and training in Tibet in the traditional way before everything changed in 1959. In his youth in Tibet he engaged in rigorous practice; in his middle years as a refugee in India he extended his studies to traditions other than his own Karma Kagyu; and later he has traveled and taught widely.

This book, *Stars of Wisdom*, contains Khenpo Rinpoche's teachings on a variety of topics, including the path of reasoning, meditation on emptiness, the songs of Milarepa, and Mahayana aspiration prayers.

It follows earlier commentaries on Nagarjuna's and Chandrakirti's classic works. I have no doubt readers wishing to cultivate the Buddhist conduct and view will find much to inspire them here.

Tenzin Gyatso
The Fourteenth Dalai Lama
May 27, 2009

The Karmapa

Foreword

WHEN WE CONSIDER the remarkable achievements of Khenpo Tsültrim Gyamtso Rinpoche and his contribution to the Dharma, he is, without doubt, one of the great guides of our time.

From a very young age he dedicated himself to the Dharma, and he has spent many years practicing diligently, following the example of other great masters of the Kagyu practice lineage.

I have always admired Rinpoche's way of training his students. His approach is direct, sincere, and uncontrived, and he is not afraid to use unorthodox methods when necessary. I find this unique and commendable. Not only has he fostered a sangha of students, he has also produced many trained translators and hence made possible the dissemination of the teachings of the Kagyu lineage in many different languages.

We arc living through turbulent times, and it is extremely difficult to find such an experienced practitioner and teacher. We are fortunate to have this great opportunity to listen to and read his teachings and commentaries and benefit from his wealth of experience.

The most important of a lama's activities is his speech, his teaching. Thus, it gives me great pleasure that efforts have been made to ensure that Rinpoche's speech activity will be preserved for future generations by the publication of this collection of his teachings.

I pray that the wisdom and experience contained in this book will benefit all who read it.

Ogyen Trinley Dorje
The Seventeenth Gyalwang Karmapa
February 24, 2009

Translators' Introduction

GREAT BUDDHIST MASTERS employ a variety of skillful methods
to guide their students on the path to enlightenment. These different
techniques both challenge and aid students to develop within themselves an array of positive qualities—qualities that can overcome
confusion and suffering, and reveal ever more brightly the wisdom
and compassion the students innately possess as the true nature of
their minds. Having different techniques to practice also helps to
ensure that a student's path of practice does not become stale or
one-dimensional. And students with different methods of practice at
their disposal can develop the ability to know which methods are
most beneficial in the many differing experiences and situations that
make up the variety of life.

Khenpo Tsültrim Gyamtso Rinpoche is a paradigm of such a great
Buddhist master. For nearly three decades before he entered semi-
retreat in 2006, Khenpo Rinpoche traveled the world teaching a varied path of Buddhist practice. This path engages students' minds in
analytical inquiry of the profound; their speech in singing songs of
realization; their bodies in yogic exercise and dance; and their hearts
in cultivating compassion and making aspiration prayers of altruism. Rinpoche's teachings are as profound as they are practical;
meaningful as they are enjoyable; direct and precise as they are spacious and compassionate.

Stars of Wisdom is a collection that conveys this range of Rinpoche's main teachings and teaching style. The book is divided into three parts: analytical meditation, songs of realization, and Mahayana aspiration prayers.

ANALYTICAL INQUIRY AND MEDITATION ON THE TRUE NATURE OF REALITY

Buddhism teaches that realizing the true nature of reality—the true nature of mind—is the key to dispelling confusion, disturbing emotions, and suffering. This true nature is as well the most profound of all things that can be known; yet, by means of the path of analytical inquiry and meditation, we *can* know and experience it.

In this part's first chapter, "The Path of Faith and the Path of Reasoning," Rinpoche introduces analytical inquiry and meditation. He begins by explaining the characteristics of religious or philosophical paths of faith and reasoning, the differences between these two paths, and how they can complement each other. Rinpoche describes the benefits of gaining faith via inquiry and analysis, because faith that proceeds from reasoning is more stable than faith that does not. He then concisely teaches how to analyze the Buddha's teachings to see if they are valid, and then how we can apply Buddhist analysis directly to finding reality's true nature within our own life experiences. This way, instead of being abstract and theoretical, analysis produces wisdom that is directly beneficial to ourselves and others.

The next chapter, "The Stages of View at the Heart of Definitive Meaning," is a text in verse that Rinpoche composed explaining the progressively subtler and more profound levels of meditation on the true nature of reality. This sequence organizes into stages the teachings and meditation instructions of Buddhism's major philosophical schools. While the Buddha himself did not specifically identify these schools, they were devised and revised by his followers based on their understanding of his teachings. But this systematic progression as taught by Khenpo Rinpoche does not emphasize discrete schools of thought with adherents rigidly fixed in competing views. Rather, it provides a step-by-step way to heighten our own individual understanding and practice.

Thus, if the Buddha's enlightenment is a lofty peak of perfect realization, the progressive stages give us the path up the mountain that we can climb in incremental steps to reach the same summit. Because this is such an important topic, Rinpoche has taught extensively on the progressive stages, and his first book was on this subject.* The root verses of *The Stages of View at the Heart of Definitive Meaning* convey each stage's essential point concisely and clearly and include a verse on the meditation method for each stage. Therefore, they are an excellent support for contemplation and meditation. This chapter also includes Rinpoche's commentary on each verse's meaning and his answers to students' questions, giving clear guidance in the progression of the view and of the meditation practices.

Songs of Realization in Dharma Practice

The second part describes a quite different yet totally complementary method of practice: songs of realization. Singing Dharma songs is an extraordinarily skillful and enjoyable Buddhist practice technique that Rinpoche has introduced to his students in a variety of ways: Rinpoche himself sings regularly; he has given illuminating explanations of the profound songs of the great masters; has composed many of his own songs; and has instructed and encouraged students to translate these songs into their own languages and sing them in their own national and cultural melodies.

This part begins with a brief introduction to the history and benefits of singing as Buddhist practice, and to Milarepa (1040–1123), Lord of Yogis, regarded in the Tibetan Buddhist tradition as one of the most accomplished masters and singers of all time.

In this part's two chapters, Rinpoche explains Milarepa's songs *The Seven Ways Things Shine Inside and Out* and *The Eighteen Kinds*

---

* Khenpo Tsültrim Gyamtso, *Progressive Stages of Meditation on Emptiness* (Oxford: Longchen Foundation, 1986).

of Yogic Joy. In the course of his teachings on these profound and wonderful songs, Rinpoche gives step-by-step instructions on how to meditate on the true nature of mind.

MAHAYANA ASPIRATION PRAYERS

In order to have a complete Dharma practice that cultivates the qualities of both mind and heart, Rinpoche has taught his students the importance of making Mahayana aspiration prayers. The "Mahayana" aspect of these aspirations is that they are motivated by altruism. For just as the variety of maladies that sentient beings suffer from is huge, so we can make aspiration prayers equally varied and vast in scope that sentient beings will be free from suffering and will enjoy the purest of happiness. We can also make aspirations that our own personal qualities of wisdom and compassion will develop so that we can be of increasing benefit to others.

This final part of the book begins with an introduction to the practice of making aspiration prayers, followed by two such aspiration prayers composed by Rinpoche himself: *Auspiciousness That Lights Up the Universe* and *A Prayer That These True Words Be Swiftly Fulfilled.*

It seems most appropriate, then, to close this introduction to *Stars of Wisdom* with an aspiration prayer: May everyone who reads this book find it of benefit, and in this way may the teachings it contains be a source of joy and peace.

Part One

Analytical Inquiry and Meditation on the True Nature of Reality

1

The Path of Faith and the Path of Reasoning

Translated by Ari Goldfield

WE CAN EXAMINE any philosophical, religious, or spiritual tradition to see what role it gives to the path of faith and what role to the path of reasoning. In a tradition where the path of faith is foremost, a practitioner first believes in the authenticity of that tradition's exponent or teacher. As a result of that faith in the teacher, one believes the teacher's words. In those traditions, the teacher is most important.

In contrast, in a tradition that emphasizes the path of reasoning, the actual teachings that are given are more important than whomever the individual teacher may be. People who follow this path use their own intelligence to examine a teacher's explanations. In the course of one's examination, one asks: "Are these teachings really an antidote for my suffering? Do they help to relieve the disturbing emotions I experience? Do they help me to clear away my confusion?" If one intelligently examines the teachings and answers these questions in the affirmative, then one will believe in the teachings and hold their exponent in high regard. Thus, gaining confidence in the teachings (and, as a result of that, gaining faith in the teacher) is the path of reasoning.

The Buddha emphasized the importance of this path of reasoning, this intelligent examination of what is being taught. He told his students that their level of faith in his teachings and in him should be a product of their own critical analysis of his words. He said that if they analyzed and found his teachings beneficial, they should practice them, and if not, they should leave them aside. In this way, people who listened to his teachings should be like a merchant buying gold: Gold merchants do not merely accept the seller's praise of his goods, but rather, they use a variety of methods to examine the quality of the merchandise before they make their purchase decision. Similarly, the Buddha said, do not accept my teachings out of faith in me, but rather, out of your own confidence in my words—confidence that you have reached as a result of your own intelligent analysis.

The noble Nagarjuna is an excellent example of a Buddhist student who proceeded in this way. This is demonstrated by the opening verse of homage to the Buddha in Nagarjuna's text *The Sixty Stanzas of Reasoning:*

To the one who has taught dependent arising,
The method we can use to abandon birth and death,
To the mighty sage, I prostrate.

Nagarjuna praises the Buddha here for his teachings. Nagarjuna says: Buddha, mighty sage, you are the one who has revealed to us the principles of dependent arising. And by having analyzed these principles, I have gained certainty in their accuracy and efficacy. I see that I can use them to cut through the net of mistaken views, abandon birth and death, and thus liberate myself from samsara's suffering. Your teachings make you a great benefactor for me and all sentient beings, and so I bow to you in homage.

This emphasis on the path of reasoning does not deny the importance of faith. Faith is vital, but the way in which one arrives at one's faith is important. When faith arises as a result of analysis, it is much more stable, because that analysis will astutely detect and be able to resolve whatever doubts one might have. In contrast, when one simply believes in something from the outset, without having used one's intelligence to analyze the reasons for holding that belief, there is the danger that later on one will become cognizant of logical contradictions to one's belief and begin to doubt it. In that instance resolving doubts is difficult, because one has deprived oneself of the tool of intelligent analysis.

That is why it is important to analyze from the outset, and to use analysis to clear up doubts. When one is analyzing and studying, it is good to ask questions and to have doubts. It is good to give one's intelligence free rein to investigate. Analysis produces a faith that is certain and that does not have to be shielded from logical inquiry or newly obtained information.

At this point, we may ask: What should we analyze, and how should we do it?

ANALYZING OUR OWN EXPERIENCE

The Buddha's teachings direct us to analyze *the mode of appearance*, meaning how something appears to be, and *the mode of underlying reality*, meaning how something actually is—its true nature.

These two modes are different; the problem comes when we do not differentiate between them. Ordinarily, sentient beings are afflicted by this confusion, which is primarily a mistaken way of thinking. We think there is no underlying reality that is different from what we think is appearing to us; we do not question the validity of the information that our thoughts give us about our experiences. This confusion is what causes sentient beings to suffer, and this experience of confusion and suffering the Buddha called *samsara*.

So samsara is basically when we think about our experiences in a confused way. However, the Buddha also taught that if we relate to our experiences with wisdom rather than ignorance, we can be free of suffering and realize the true nature of our mind. This the Buddha called *nirvana*.

This presentation is quite contrary to our habitual way of thinking about things, so we should not take it at face value—we need to investigate it. And we can see that this investigation should focus on our very own experience. How does our experience appear to be? What is its true nature? That is what we must use our intelligence to investigate and analyze.

We should start by analyzing the state of existence that we find ourselves in right now. When we consider what constitutes our existence, we find that it is quite simply our six consciousnesses—the eye, ear, nose, tongue, body, and mental consciousnesses; and the six kinds of objects that appear to those six consciousnesses—visual forms, sounds, odors, tastes, bodily sensations, and mental phenomena. This is what we experience when we are alive: sense perceptions and their objects, and thoughts and the objects of those thoughts.

DIRECT COGNITION VERSUS THOUGHTS' ABSTRACTIONS

We can begin our analysis with the basic and familiar experience of our eyes seeing forms. When that visual perception occurs, what is the true nature of the form that is the eye-sense-consciousness's focal object? What is the true nature of the eye-sense-faculty that supports the perception? And what is the nature of the consciousness supported by that sense faculty? In terms of the mode of appearance, how does the eye-sense-consciousness perceive its object? And what is the perception's mode of underlying reality? We need to examine both the mode of appearance and the mode of underlying reality here. When we analyze our own sense faculties, sense consciousnesses, and their focal objects like this, we make our very own experience the subject of our analysis, and this makes the analysis both immediate and profound.

To apply this analysis right here and now, let us look together out the big window to my left at an orange growing on the tree outside. We see that orange with our eyes, but actually it appears differently to each of our six consciousnesses. This is true for any entity—it has six different modes of appearance. So for the eye-sense-consciousness, the only focal objects that appear are the orange's shape and color—the orange's other qualities do not manifest. For the ear-sense-consciousness, all that appears is the sound that the orange makes when it falls from the tree and hits the ground, or the sound it makes when you peel its skin. The orange's form does not and cannot appear to the ear-sense-consciousness; the ear-sense-consciousness does not have the ability to engage the orange's form. The nose-sense-consciousness only perceives the quality of the orange's scent; the orange's other qualities do not appear to it. The tongue-sense-consciousness only perceives the quality of the orange's taste, how sweet and how tangy it is. The body-sense-consciousness only perceives the sensation of how the orange feels when it contacts the body; the orange's form, sound, smell, and taste do not appear to it. Thus, each of the five sense consciousnesses only perceives its own specific object.

What, then, appears to the sixth consciousness, the mental consciousness? In other words, what focal object appears to our thoughts? The conceptual mental consciousness cannot perceive the orange's form, sound, smell, taste, or bodily sensation. Instead, a thought can only impute an abstract image. This abstract image is neither form, sound, smell, taste, nor bodily sensation. A thought imputes that abstract, unclear, indirect image, attaches the name "orange" to it, and thinks that it is actually perceiving the orange, when in fact it is not.

This is the important point to recognize: Thoughts do not perceive anything directly; they cannot perceive the actual, unique object. They can only impute generalities and unclear abstractions. In contrast, the five sense consciousnesses do directly perceive specific things, but they do not make conceptual judgments about them.

When we consider the mode of appearance in this way, we see that one orange appears in five different ways to each of the five sense-consciousnesses, and that the conceptual mental consciousness (our thoughts) only perceives the abstract image of its own conceptual imputation. We mistakenly believe that when we think "orange," the orange that is the object of our thoughts is one and the same as the orange we see, hear, smell, taste, and touch. But the underlying reality is that the "orange" that is the object of our thoughts cannot be seen, heard, smelled, tasted, or touched. It is just a facet of our imagination. Thus, analysis allows us to easily understand that the mode of appearance and the mode of underlying reality are different.

Then we can also examine other qualities of this orange. For example, it is created by causes and conditions—it is a composite result of many different causes and conditions coming together. Therefore, it is something that is constantly changing as the causes and conditions that act upon it change. It arises and ceases moment by moment, and so whatever is there in one moment, by the next moment has ceased: it has the quality of impermanence. Also, since it is only the product of causes and conditions, it has no nature of its own; no truly independent identity; it does not inherently exist. Thus, it is said to have the quality of emptiness. Impermanence and emptiness are qualities of the orange's underlying reality, its true nature.

However, our ordinary thoughts simply think "orange," and these thoughts impute permanence and substantial existence to that abstract image they have of the orange. Our thoughts cling to true existence and do not recognize the qualities of impermanence and emptiness. So again, we can see how the mode of what appears to our thoughts and the mode of underlying reality are different.

This important distinction reveals the confusion that causes us suffering. For example, when our thoughts believe that an entity is permanent, that is a mistake, and that mistake causes us to suffer. Because when we believe an entity that makes us happy is permanent, we suffer when that entity ceases to exist. And when we believe an entity that makes us suffer is permanent, we deny ourselves the relief of knowing that it is impermanent and will therefore not cause us suffering forever, or even close to it!

So the more certainty we have that our thoughts' projections are mistaken, the less we will blindly believe they are true, and the better off we will be.

DIRECT PERCEPTION, THOUGHTS, AND TIME

Let us examine the difference between sense consciousnesses' perceptions and thoughts with regard to time. The five sense consciousnesses are nonconceptual, which means that they do not think one way or another about the objects they perceive. Therefore, the five sense consciousnesses directly perceive the unique forms, sounds, odors, tastes, and bodily sensations that exist only in the present moment. With the sense consciousnesses there are no past and future, because there is only the perception of what is right here, right now.

In contrast, thoughts do look at the past and future. However, the past has ceased, so it does not exist; and the future has not arisen, so it does not exist either. Thus, when thoughts look at the past and future, they are looking at nonexistence; at an absence of any particular thing. Therefore, only an abstract image of the past and future, which thoughts themselves have imputed, can appear to thoughts. We spend a lot of time thinking and worrying about the past and the future, but this analysis shows us that this past and future are merely our own thoughts' creation; past and future do not actually exist.

The five sense consciousnesses only look at the present. From the time we were young children until now, the objects perceived by the five sense consciousnesses have only been the unique objects of the present moment. The sense consciousnesses have never looked at the past or the future.

Yesterday's sense consciousnesses perceived yesterday's unique forms, sounds, odors, tastes, and bodily sensations; they do not perceive today's unique objects. Today's sense consciousnesses only look at today's unique objects; they do not look at the unique objects that existed yesterday, nor do they perceive the unique objects of tomorrow. Tomorrow's sense consciousnesses will only perceive tomorrow's unique objects; they will not look at the unique objects of yesterday and today—how could they?

It is just like watching a movie. When you watch a movie for two hours, your eye-sense-consciousness actually only ever sees each instant of the unique object of the movie that exists in the present; it never sees the past or the future. Even though it is like that, even though all that actually exists is the entity that exists in the present moment, thoughts lump past, present, and future entities together and falsely believe that they are one continuously existent thing.

Take the example of one of our hands in three different states: First we make a fist, second we move our hand about, and finally we let our fingers relax out of the clenched fist. The eye-sense-consciousness that perceives the fist, the eye-sense-consciousness that perceives the fist moving, and the eye-sense-consciousness that perceives the hand in its relaxed state are different from each other. The same eye-sense-consciousness does not perceive all these things together. The reason for this is that when the hand is first held steady in a fist, its movement does not appear; when it is moving, its stillness does not appear; and when it is relaxed, the fist held steady and the fist in motion do not appear. So how could the eye-sense-consciousness in one moment that perceives one image but not the others be the same as the eye-sense-consciousnesses that do perceive the others?

We can also analyze and see that the five sense consciousnesses do not label or cling to the names of what they perceive. When the eye-sense-consciousness perceives the hand, it does not grasp at the labels "fist," "moving," or "relaxed"; it does not even think "hand." It perceives the images of these three phases, but does not attach names to them. The reason for this is that the unique object has neither names nor labels, and therefore the consciousness that directly perceives the unique object is nonconceptual.

In contrast, thoughts cling to the three images as being one thing. Thoughts give the same label "hand" to the three different objects appearing to the three different eye-sense-consciousnesses—they think that the name "hand" and those three objects are the same thing. "What is moving there is my hand; the fist is also my hand; and when relaxed out of a clenched fist, that is also my hand." Thoughts confusedly lump these three phases together and cling to them as being one thing, even though they are not one and the same thing at all.

Now, examine your own mode of appearance and mode of underlying reality: How do your sense consciousnesses and thoughts perceive you? From the time you were young children until now, your five sense consciousnesses have never regarded you with any clinging. They have simply perceived their own unique objects without clinging to them in any way. Your thoughts are what cling to there being one unchanging self from your childhood to the present. You do think that from childhood until now, you have been just one person, right? You think, "When I was young, I was like this and that; now I am like this and that," but you still think that the "me" of the past is the same as the "me" of the present. Thoughts look at these different moments and confusedly believe that they are one thing. Thoughts cling in that way, not the five sense consciousnesses.

Let us return to the orange and connect it with this examination: With this one orange, there is the orange of the past, the orange of the present, and the orange of the future. However, when thoughts conceive of the orange, they lump these together into one. So for example when thoughts think of the orange as smelling sweet, they do not think of the past orange, the present orange, and the future orange; rather, they lump them all together into one. And when we think not of this particular orange, but just of an orange in general, we take all the oranges in the world that ever have been and ever will be and confuse them together into one. We cling to all those oranges as just being one, but the image of the orange that arises in our minds is not clear. It is only an abstraction. That is all that thoughts can conceive of—unclear abstractions. Yet thoughts label those abstractions as "good" and "bad," "pleasant" and "unpleasant," and then thoughts believe that the labels truly exist in the objects. Thoughts believe the objects really are good or bad, even though the sense consciousnesses do not perceive those labels of "good" and "bad" at all.

If we still have doubts, we may ask: "What proof is there that the five sense consciousnesses are nonconceptual?" We can know this from what happens when we meditate. When we abide in meditation and our minds remain free of thoughts, then our eyes may see forms and our ears may hear sounds, but thoughts do not arise. Clinging to names and labels does not arise. That is one sign that the five sense consciousnesses are nonconceptual. Another sign is that when you

see a person for the first time, you do not know their name. That is
because your eye-consciousness perceives the person's form, but it
does not conceive of anything about her. You should investigate and
find other examples that demonstrate how the five sense consciousnesses are nonconceptual. Then see how your thoughts conceive of
so many different labels and judgments about the objects that your
sense consciousnesses perceive nonconceptually, and notice the different emotional reactions arising as a result.

ANALYSIS AND THE REALIZATION OF EQUALITY

The Buddha emphasized this way of analyzing the mode of appearance and the mode of underlying reality as a method for carrying
oneself out of confusion and into enlightenment. That is why the
divisions of the Buddha's teachings are called *yanas*, meaning
"vehicles"—the vehicles we use to carry us on this journey to realization. There are different presentations of how many yanas there
are—sometimes three, sometimes nine; once the Buddha even taught
that there is a different yana for each different concept we have, because each concept contains an element of confusion that we need to
know how to transcend.

However, the Buddha also taught that although all of these different yanas and their philosophical presentations appear to exist, ultimately there is only one vehicle, because we ourselves only have one
true nature, not many.

That ultimate vehicle is equality. Equality means that contradictions, opposites, differences, and distinctions appear but do not truly
exist. In the true nature of reality, opposites, differences, and distinctions are undifferentiable; they are equality.

It is important for you to analyze appearances and see for yourself
whether their true nature is equality or not. You can start by analyzing yourself. Ordinarily when you look at yourself, you think "self."
But when others look at you, they do not think of you as "self," they
think of you as "other." So who are you? Are you "self" or "other"? In

genuine reality, self and other are equality. You are actually neither self nor other—you are the equality of self and other.

Generally, the identities of "self" and "other" depend on concepts. Without concepts, there would be neither self nor other. Earth and stones are not self and other, nor do they conceive of them. So when you are "myself" or "me," that depends upon concepts, and more specifically, upon your own individual concepts. When you are "other," that is in dependence upon the concepts of all other sentient beings besides yourself. When you reflect in this way, you can see how you are also "other," and how all others are also "me," because all sentient beings think of themselves in the same way. Therefore, when we ask, "Who is really self, and who is really other?" the answer is that self and other are actually equality.

Next, we can ask ourselves, "Are we 'friend,' 'enemy,' or neither friend nor enemy?" The answer is that we are the equality of friend and enemy. Because from the perspective of our enemies' thoughts, we are enemy; from the perspective of those whose thoughts cling to us as "friend," we are friend; and for those who are neutral toward us, we are neither friend nor enemy. So what are we genuinely? It is impossible to define exactly what we are. And that demonstrates that our true nature is equality.

If because some sentient beings think of us as "enemy," we would also think of ourselves as an enemy, that would be incorrect because many others think of us as "friend." However, if because some people think of us as a friend, we also thought "I am a friend," that would be incorrect because there are those who think of us as an enemy. If, in dependence upon the thoughts in the minds of those who are neutral toward us, we thought of ourselves as neither friend nor enemy, that would be incorrect because in dependence upon the minds of our friends and enemies we do in fact become one or the other. Therefore, our own true nature is equality.

We may also wonder, "Am I a good person or a bad person?" The answer that our thoughts will give us will not be stable. Sometimes, when our bodies are healthy and our minds are free from suffering and at ease, we think, "I am good. I am a fine person." However, when things are difficult, we begin to think, "I am bad." So we cannot rely on our thoughts to tell us if we are good or bad. In fact, our thoughts about whether we are good or bad can change quickly. So if we cannot rely on our own thoughts, can we rely on others for a judgment on this? If we do, we will find that some people think we are good, while others think we are bad. This shows that in the true nature of reality, good and bad are equality. We are neither truly a good person nor a bad one—whether we ourselves are a good person or a bad person is equality.

When we analyze our bodies, we notice that we consume a lot of food. So, can we objectively be called a "consumer"? No, our body is not a 100 percent consumer, because many insects and parasites consume it. In India and Nepal in the summertime, many tens of thousands of mosquitoes bite people from head to toe. There, one's body becomes a giant piece of food. So from one perspective, our bodies are consumers of food, and from another perspective they are food that is consumed. Since we cannot say whether our bodies are definitively "consumer" or "consumed," our bodies are equality.

We can also ask, are our bodies residents or residences? Superficially, you may think that you are a resident because you live in a residence—you are not a residence yourself. However, many tiny creatures live in our bodies, so actually you are a residence. Since you cannot say decisively that your body is a resident or a residence, your body is equality.

Why is it important to analyze these things? Because we suffer greatly from believing that "self," "other," "good," "bad," and all other conceptually imputed labels, differences, and contradictions truly exist. But when we understand that the true nature of reality is equality, it is easy to see the difference between that true nature and the merely relative, superficial appearances of differences and contradictions. And since in the true nature, differences and contradictions do not exist, it is inherently free of conflict. The true nature is at peace, open, spacious, and relaxed.

So let us apply this analysis to our environment as well—first, to our planet. Wherever we are on this planet, we think that we are on the top of the planet, right-side-up. If anyone had the thought that they were on the bottom of the planet, upside-down, they would feel as though they were going to fall off! For example, those of us here in America think we are right-side-up and that Australia is "down under," but Australians do not fall off the planet. They think that they are right-side-up too. So everyone thinks that they are on top of the planet, right-side-up. However, if there is no upside-down at all, there cannot possibly be any right-side-up either. Therefore, right-side-up and upside-down are equality; top and bottom are equality; and the appearances of right-side-up, upside-down, top, and bottom, are merely conceptual. They do not truly exist. On our planet, direction is equality.

We should also consider space itself—the space that surrounds our planet and encompasses all the stars and planets there are. What we find is that space just goes on and on—it has no end. And since space has no end, it also has no center, no midpoint. Since space in reality has neither center nor end, center and end are equality. And in space without center or end, there is no way to actually go anywhere, because coming and going require the reference points of location, of center and end. Therefore, coming and going are also equality.

What about our experiences of happiness and suffering? Are they equality too? This is perhaps the most important question to consider. In fact, happiness and suffering are equality because when we analyze them, we find that they cannot exist from their own side; rather, they exist only in dependence upon each other.

Suffering depends upon its reference point of happiness—if happiness did not exist at all, neither would suffering. In the same way, happiness exists only in dependence upon suffering. If we never suffered, we would not know what happiness is. Even the word "happiness" would have no meaning. So if there were no experience of suffering, there would be no experience of happiness, and if there were no word "suffering," there would be no word "happiness."

Since happiness and suffering are dependently existent in this way, they are not truly existent. They are like happiness and suffering in a dream. We may dream of attending a party in a beautiful garden filled with flowers on a calm, lovely day, and of feeling very happy to be there. However, if the weather turns bad, gusts of wind begin to blow the leaves off the trees and even the trees fall over, in dependence upon the earlier mere appearance of happiness, thoughts of its opposite, suffering, would arise. Since both happiness and suffering can only exist one in dependence upon the other, neither one can be truly existent. It is easy to understand how they do not exist in a dream, and that is why the dream example is given.

Then based on the dream example, one can think about how it is during the waking state. Attending parties and many other events can cause the appearance of happiness to arise in our minds. But the only reason we can know that we are happy is that we have had the experience of suffering. This is what is meant by dependent existence: All opposites depend for their existence upon each other in this same way, and therefore opposites do not truly exist; opposites are equality.

The benefit of our knowing that opposites are equality, particularly opposites like "happiness" and "suffering," "friend" and "enemy," and "good" and bad," is that we stop clinging to opposites as being truly existent. We stop hoping so much for one alternative and fearing its opposite; we stop worrying about which one will appear and which one will not. We begin to be able to regard opposites with spacious and relaxed equanimity.

THE ROLE OF MEDITATION

When you experience acute suffering, like a powerful physical illness or intense mental anguish, it may seem as though the logical analyses we have just discussed are not very strong, because they can seem to be a rather weak remedy in the face of the trauma you are experiencing.

However, it is not that these analyses lack power, it is that your clinging to the true existence of what is troubling you is so strong. Your view of how appearances are not truly existent is not strong enough yet. You need to strengthen your certainty in equality by con-templating it and analyzing it until you have removed all your doubts about it. When your view of the true nature is strong, it can over-come all suffering, no matter how great. It is like a dream: You can dream of being very sick, of taking medicine, even of going to the hospital; but the moment you recognize you are dreaming, you rec-ognize that your sickness is a mere appearance, and your suffering immediately decreases.

Meditation will also help to make your view stronger. Meditation does not necessarily mean that you have to be seated on a cushion. It means that you cultivate your certainty in equality by recalling it briefly, again and again throughout the day. Then you rest relaxed within that certainty. You can do that on a cushion or during daily activities.

When we meditate we have different experiences. Sometimes our meditation goes well, and we experience clarity, spaciousness, and bliss; other times, our minds have unpleasant experiences during meditation. At first, we may have a lot of hopes and fears with regard to positive and negative meditation experiences, but we need to make our hopes and fears smaller and smaller, until we have transcended hope and fear completely.

At the same time, the way to transcend hope and fear is not to block it, cut it off, or to try to prevent it from arising. Rather, the way to transcend hope and fear is to meditate on hope and fear's true nature. For example, in the great master Gotsangpa's song *The Seven Delights*, he sings:

When thoughts that there is something, perceived and a perceiver,
Lure my mind away and distract,
I don't close my senses' gateways to meditate without them
But plunge straight into their essential point.
They're like clouds in the sky, there's this shimmer where they fly;
Thoughts that rise, for me sheer delight!*

* *Translated under the guidance of Khenpo Tsültrim Gyamtso Rinpoche by Jim Scott and Anne Burchardi, 1996.*

That is the Mahamudra meditation style: When thoughts fill the mind, one does not regard them as unpleasant, because one can look directly at their true nature and relax within that. As the Lord Gampopa has taught: "Consider thoughts to be necessary; consider thoughts to be very kind; consider thoughts to be pleasant; consider thoughts to be indispensable."* Since thoughts' true nature is Dharmata, the essential nature of reality, they are pleasant. If one did not have any thoughts, one could not meditate. Therefore, in Mahamudra meditation, one even intentionally produces thoughts so that one can meditate on their true nature.

Concerning the sense consciousnesses, Mahamudra meditation regards sense perception as one would in a lucid dream: If one recognizes one is dreaming and one simply remains undistracted from that awareness, one does not have to shut off sense perceptions.

The first turning of the wheel of Dharma's instructions are to shut off sense perceptions while meditating. The reason for this is that if one clings to outer appearances as being truly existent, when one perceives appearances, attachment and aversion arise.

However, the view of *The Transcendent Wisdom Sutras* (Skt.: *Prajnaparamita Sutras*) of the middle turning of the wheel of Dharma is that outer appearances are like dreams. When you know this, you do not have to prevent appearances from manifesting to your sense consciousnesses. When you are able to cultivate awareness of the illusory, dreamlike nature of appearances, that is called the "illusion-like samadhi." Meditating in this samadhi is important.

When we follow the path of reasoning, we use our intelligence to critically examine what our teachers explain to us. We resolve our doubts about their teachings by analyzing our own life experiences to see if the teachings are valid and give useful insights. If we can gain certainty in the teachings' accuracy and benefit, we meditate in order to turn that certainty into experience of the true nature of reality.

* Quoted in Karmapa Wangchuk Dorje's guide to Mahamudra meditation titled *The Ocean of the Definitive Meaning* (Tib.: *phyag chen nges don rgya mtsho*) (Rumtek, India), Tibetan folios 90f–b.

This has positive effects—you should investigate for yourself and see. Then you will have a faith that comes from your own intelligence and diligence, rather than from an external command. It will not be faith in an outer person or doctrine; it will be faith in your own true nature—faith that is inseparable from the true nature of your mind.

2

The Stages of View at the Heart of Definitive Meaning

TRANSLATED BY ROSE TAYLOR

> To the Buddha, the supreme teacher, the Mighty One,
> And to the perfectly wise and powerful Manjushri
> I pay homage with great respect.
> I shall now explain the stages of view of definitive meaning. (1)*

IT IS TRADITIONAL to begin a Buddhist text with an homage and commitment to the text's composition. The first three lines of this verse are the opening homage, and the fourth is the commitment to compose this text.

THE SELFLESSNESS OF THE INDIVIDUAL

All Buddhist traditions consider it important to understand the self-lessness of the individual in order to gain liberation from suffering. The reason for this is that all suffering comes from believing the self is truly existent. For example, when we think "I am angry," "I am

* Verse numbers correspond to the numbers of the Tibetan verses in Khenpo Rinpoche's original composition, *The Stages of View at the Heart of Definitive Meaning*. The verses Rinpoche spontaneously composed in the course of explaining this text and answering questions about it do not have verse numbers.

afraid," or "I am in pain," we suffer because we believe this "I" is truly existent. This results in taking the self and everything that affects it very seriously, and we become fixated on pursuing happiness and avoiding suffering. But in fact, the self does not truly exist; it is appearance-emptiness, like the self that appears in a dream. This is called "the selflessness of the individual."

In order to understand this selflessness, it is first necessary to investigate what we consider to be the self. Most people have a strong sense of having a personal self that is distinct from everything that is different from it—namely, the external world and other people. However, it is unusual for us to examine what this entity of a self actually is. When we investigate our experience of self, we find that we believe the self to have three qualities: permanence, singularity, and independence.

First, we think the self is permanent. This does not mean that we consider ourselves to be immortal, because we certainly know that at some point we will die. Nevertheless, we behave as if the self has some lasting duration from one moment to the next. If we believed that the self dissolved moment-by-moment, we would not be so deeply concerned with it. The self has to be continuous in order for us to fixate on it as we do when we try to ensure that we accumulate things that it likes and shield it from what it dislikes. For example, we work hard to amass money and possessions that we can use in the future. Or when we feel injured by someone else, we carry that with us, thinking: "You hurt me last week." These types of actions and thoughts are clearly founded on the assumption that the self is the same self from past to present to future. If we considered the future self to be different from the present self, we would not feel the need to strive so hard to benefit and protect it. Therefore, we see that in our experience, we behave as if this self is permanent, because we believe it is continuous, of lasting duration.

Second, we think that the self is singular. Each individual believes that they have one self. Even though there are many different body parts and mental experiences, we consider all of those aspects to be bound together as one single self. If we did not view the self in this way, we would think we had many selves, but that is not our experience.

Lastly, we consider the self to be independent. Each of us thinks that we control our own movements and actions in the world and that we exist in and of ourselves, distinct from whatever else there might be in the world.

Thus, when we look at our own experience, we see that we believe the self truly exists as a permanent, single, and independent entity. And since our belief that this self truly exists is what creates our suffering, the Buddha taught us to examine the self to see if it really does exist or not. If it is causing so many problems for us, it makes sense to investigate it and figure out how to resolve these difficulties.

So let us look for this self that we believe to exist. Where should we look? All the phenomena that make up our experience are subsumed within the categories of mind and matter, so let us look for the self there. In order to help us look in a more systematic and organized way, the Buddha further classified mind and matter into five groups known as the five aggregates.

We need to analyze these five aggregates to see if we can find a permanent, single, independent self within them. The first aggregate is that of forms, which includes all material phenomena that are perceivable by the five sense consciousnesses (the eye-, ear-, nose-, tongue-, and body-sense-consciousnesses). The remaining four aggregates—feelings, discriminations, formations, and consciousnesses—are all categories of mind.

The Aggregate of Forms Is Not the Self

Even though we believe the body is the self,
There is no "body" that possesses its parts.
And because there are many parts,
When we examine with reasoning, we know the body is not
    the self. (2)

The aggregate of forms comprises all material phenomena; for sentient beings it refers to the individual's body. The perception of a self arises in relation to our body; we cling to this body of ours as being "me." However, if we investigate with authentic wisdom that analyzes for ultimate selflessness, we find that the body is not the self.

The reason for this is that the body is not a substantial thing; "body" is just a name given to a collection of many parts. One cannot find any entity of the body that is the possessor of these various parts. One finds the parts themselves, like the arms, legs, and so forth, but since other than these parts, no entity of a body can be found, the body is not the self.

Furthermore, the collection of parts is not the self. If it were, then when we lost a part of the collection—for example, when we have a tooth removed—then the concept of the self would also be lost. However, this is not our experience; we maintain our sense of self despite what happens to the collection of body parts.

The only alternative way for the body's parts to be the self would be if each part were the self. However, if each of the parts of the body were the self, there would have to be an equal number of selves as there are parts of the body.

Thus, when we examine our habitual assumptions about the self and analyze to see whether or not they are accurate, we find that the body is not the self. While in common worldly consensus we converse in terms that assume our self is found in our body, there is no ultimate reality to that situation. When we realize that the body is not the self, but rather is just the momentary coming together of causes and conditions, we may still take care of it in order to have a functioning body that is useful to us, but we do not need to be overly concerned with what happens to it.

We can see that whatever happens to this body is like what happens to a dream body in a dream world. If our body is carried away by water or eaten by a tiger in a dream when we know we are dreaming, then we are not upset by what is happening because there is no truly existent self that is undergoing these experiences. Then, even when we appear to experience great suffering, we can relax. We might even enjoy the novelty of being eaten by a dream tiger.

THE AGGREGATE OF FEELINGS IS NOT THE SELF

If pleasant feelings were the self,
When great suffering arose, the self would be destroyed.
If painful feelings were the self,
When great pleasure arose, the self would be destroyed.
When we examine well like this,
We know that feelings are not the self. (3)

The second aggregate, the aggregate of feelings, is the collection of our experiences that we find pleasant, unpleasant, or neutral. While we do not consciously think of our self as merely "sadness" or any other feeling, we often associate ourselves closely with our emotional state. We define who we are with such statements as "I am happy" or "I am sad." It can be hard to separate our sense of self from what we are currently feeling, and emotions can seem uncontrollable and overwhelming.

So let us examine feelings to see if they really are the self. If pleasant feelings were the self, the nature of the self would be pleasant feelings. For there to be a self there would have to be pleasant feelings; if suffering arose, the self would cease to exist because there would be no pleasant feelings to constitute the self. Conversely, if the self were painful feelings, there would have to be suffering for there to be a self, and when joy arose, the self would be destroyed. Therefore, when one excellently examines with wisdom, it becomes clear that feelings are not the self.

When we repeatedly contemplate this verse, we gain certainty that feelings are not the self. And when we have this certainty, we are no longer so overwhelmed by our feelings because they do not define us. As we experience feelings as less solid and stuck, they become softer and more dreamlike. Whatever emotion arises, we can relax. We do not need to try to hold onto it, or to push it away.

THE AGGREGATE OF DISCRIMINATIONS IS NOT THE SELF

Since discriminating thoughts, in their great variety,
Alternate like day and night

And are dependent on the three times
When examined by the wise,
It is easily understood that they are not the self. (4)

The aggregate of discriminations is defined as the mental activity of
clinging to characteristics. It is all of our thoughts of characteristics,
or attributes, such as clean or dirty, hot or cold, and good or bad. We
habitually ascribe characteristics to objects: Seeing a cockroach, we
might label it as "dirty" and "gross"; seeing a flower, we might label it
as "beautiful" and "delicate." However, our thoughts do this so quickly
and regularly that we do not realize that these characteristics do not
exist in the objects themselves; it is just our own thoughts that are
assigning the characteristics to the objects. We mistakenly assume
that these characteristics we have thought of are intrinsic to the
objects themselves.

Not only do we do this with external objects, we also do it to ourselves. When we have thoughts such as "I am bad" or "I am right,"
then we conflate this sense of badness or rightness with the self. We
identify these particular characteristics as the self. This causes disturbing emotions to arise: Thinking "I am bad" leads to sadness and
discouragement, and thinking "I am right" leads to pride. Then when
we are discouraged, we suffer, and when we interact with the world
with pride and we are not regarded with the esteem that we think we
deserve, we suffer.

However, when the wise thoroughly analyze, they know that discriminating thoughts in their great variety are not the self. This is
because such thoughts alternate and change like the continual revo-
lution of day and night. The thought that someone is a friend changes
into the thought that they are an enemy, and then back again. The
thought of something as clean changes into the thought that it is
dirty, and back. And the thought of ourselves as good changes into
the thought of ourselves as bad, and back. Thus, discriminations are
impermanent, so they cannot be the self.

Furthermore, discriminating thoughts depend on the three
times—the past, present, and future. When we analyze, we see that

there is no past discrimination, as it has already ceased; there is no present discrimination, as the present moment does not abide for even an instant; and there is no future discrimination, as it has not yet arisen. If the self truly existed, it would have to be permanent throughout the three times; since discriminations constantly arise and cease, they are impermanent and there is no self found within discriminations.

We should contemplate well how our own discriminations have changed over time. Perhaps we considered someone an enemy and now they are our friend. When we considered them an enemy, this helped to define us. If a friend of ours becomes a friend of our enemy, we feel betrayed. The idea that someone we consider a friend thinks of our enemy as a friend challenges us and we may even decide that the person we considered a friend is now also an enemy. The fact that friend and enemy can change illustrates how discriminations change.

We should examine how our discriminations have changed progressively since we were children. The things we enjoyed as a child are probably not the same things we appreciate as an adult. If we contemplate this based on our own experience, then we can clearly see how our discriminating thoughts are continually shifting. When we stop fixating on our discriminations as being the self, we can relax.

Understanding this can help us in our relationships with other people. When someone does something we dislike, we attribute certain characteristics to them, such as "greedy" or "selfish." That event and those labels become fused with the person in our mind. The next time we see them we remember those characteristics rather than seeing them as they are in this new moment. The person recalled by our mind seems more real than the person standing in front of us. We do not even notice what this person is doing in this present moment because we are recalling the last time we saw them, and all those strong feelings come back to us, including even anger. In this way we keep our relationship frozen in our limiting labels rather than being open to changing circumstances.

At times we even do this to ourselves. For example, when we make a mistake and think, "I am sloppy and incapable," we feel very bad

about ourselves. However, we could just see that mistake as one particular instance, set the intention to be more conscientious in the
future, and not consider the mistake to define who we are. We can
learn from our mistakes without generating negative thoughts about
ourselves and becoming discouraged.

Therefore, when we examine discriminating thoughts, our daily
lives are benefited and we develop our understanding of ultimate
truth. Those with wisdom investigate discriminations and easily discover that they are not the self. In the past our discriminating thoughts
have changed a lot, and in the future our discriminating thoughts
will change a lot. When all of these discriminations dissolve, we will
be close to buddhahood.

THE AGGREGATE OF FORMATIONS IS NOT THE SELF

Examples of contradictory mental formations are
Faith and lack of faith, shame and lack of shame;
Since there are many such incompatible mental formations
Mental formations are also not the self. (5)

The aggregate of formations includes all the other thoughts and
emotions we experience that are not included in feelings and discriminations. They include mental constructions such as: faith, lack
of faith, shame, lack of shame, motivation, laziness, pride, embar-
rassment, forgetfulness, and concentration.

If these mental formations were the self, they would all have to be
the self together. However, many of these mental formations are
contradictory, and therefore they cannot exist together. For example, faith cannot exist together with lack of faith, and shame cannot
exist with lack of shame because they are opposites—they cancel
each other out. Since the mental formations cannot even exist together, they cannot be the self. And as with feelings, no one mental
formation can be the self, for if it were, as soon as it ceased, so would
the self.

When one clings to these mental formations as the self, one suf-
fers. For example, if one thinks one has faith and that is one's self,

then one thinks "I am a good person." This seems like a real situation and a real self. Later, when one feels a lack of faith, one becomes concerned and disappointed with oneself. So equating the self with these formations that change and are contradictory increases suffering. Sometimes we feel good about our thoughts and emotions and sometimes we feel bad about them—we go up and down. However, if we realize that actually these mental formations are not the self, then we do not have to go up and down with them. We can just relax.

In the Vajrayana tradition, the deity Vajrayogini wears a garland of fifty-one human heads and these symbolize the severing of the fifty-one mental formations, which means cutting through the thought that these formations are the self. When you practice Vajrayana, it is important to know the meaning of symbols such as these.

THE AGGREGATE OF CONSCIOUSNESSES IS NOT THE SELF

If the five sense consciousnesses were the self,
They would permanently perceive their objects.
Since even the mental consciousness
Is divided among the three times, none of these are the self. (6)

The aggregate of consciousnesses refers to the six primary consciousnesses that perceive their respective objects: the eye-sense-consciousness that perceives forms, the ear-sense-consciousness that perceives sounds, the nose-sense-consciousness that perceives smells, the tongue-sense-consciousness that perceives tastes, the body-sense-consciousness that perceives bodily sensations, and the mental consciousness that perceives mental objects.

We identify ourselves with our sense consciousnesses when, for example, our eye-sense-consciousness sees something and we think: "I see a form." If we think that sense experience is truly existent and that the one who experiences it is truly existent, that can cause us to suffer.

Perception of an object is the coming together of three components—the sense object, the sense faculty, and the sense consciousness. For example, seeing a blue flower involves the following components: the perceived external object; the blue flower; the eye-sense faculty that supports mind's perception of the blue flower; and the eye-sense-consciousness that actually perceives the blue flower. In order to perceive the blue flower all three of these elements are necessary.

Furthermore, a sense consciousness arises and ceases together with the object that it perceives. For example, the eye-sense-consciousness specifically perceiving a blue flower arises and ceases with the perceived blue flower. The eye-sense-consciousness perceiving some other object is not the same eye-sense-consciousness. For example, the eye-sense-consciousness perceiving a blue flower is not the same thing as the eye-sense-consciousness perceiving a stone. Even the eye-sense-consciousness perceiving a blue flower in one moment is not the same entity as the eye-sense-consciousness perceiving a blue flower in the next moment, because the flower subtly changes every moment as it goes through the change of gradual decay. So, all the sense consciousnesses arise and cease momentarily with their objects that also arise and cease momentarily.

For this reason, the sense consciousnesses are said to be impermanent. If they were the self, however, they would have to be permanent; they could never change and their objects could never change. Since that is clearly not the case, the sense consciousnesses are not the self.

The mental consciousness is the last place we can look for the self within the aggregates. We cling to the mental consciousness as being a continuous entity that knows or experiences our whole life, and this is a very strong habit. The mistake here is that we take the series of moments of the mental consciousness and blur them together to create the illusion of a permanent self.

This is like taking different moments of a river to be the same river. Let us say you go to a river one year, take your shoes off, place them on a rock by the side of the river, and suddenly the water carries the shoes away. When you return to this river a year later, you say, "This is the river that swept away my shoes." But this river is a completely different river from the one it was a few moments ago, let alone a year ago. We see that the river is continuously moving and changing but we blur all those moments of the river into one entity.

We do the same when we cling to the mental consciousness as the self. We take all these different moments of our mind's continuum, fuse them together, and call this the self. However, the mental consciousness is not the self because it occurs in the three times. Time is separated into three distinct periods: the past, present, and future. The past mental consciousness has ceased, so it does not exist. The present mental consciousness does not abide for a single instant; it ceases moment-by-moment. And the future mental consciousness has not yet arisen. Therefore, the mental consciousness is not one single, permanent entity, so it is not the self.

The Necessity for Meditating on Selflessness

In this way, it is confused to think
The five aggregates are the self.
So, in order to cut clinging to self at the root,
Meditate on selflessness, the abiding nature of reality. (7)

All sentient beings believe there is a self, but when we actually look for the self in the five aggregates that comprise body and mind, we cannot find it. "I," "me," and "mine" are convenient terms and useful in daily life, but when we cling to the self as being truly existent, many problems arise. We suffer greatly based on this confused and mistaken idea. In order to cut through the root of thoughts that believe in a truly existent self, it is necessary to meditate on selflessness.

The Way to Meditate on Selflessness

In order to gain knowledge about the abiding nature of reality,
Know that the five aggregates are not the self
And that the mind believing in the self is not the self, either,
And when you gain certainty in this, rest right within that. (8)

To meditate on selflessness, you first need to gain certainty in selflessness. So, carefully read these verses that explain selflessness and contemplate their meaning. Gradually, you will gain certainty that because the five aggregates are multiple, impermanent, and dependently arisen, the five aggregates are not the self. Look also at the mind that believes in the self—the mind that thinks "I" and "me." It is impermanent and dependently arisen as well, so it is not the self either.

When certainty in selflessness has arisen, you are ready to meditate. During your meditation session, you can recite the verses in order to refresh your certainty. When your certainty is clear, then rest the mind right within that knowledge that there is no self.

If your mind wanders, recall the certainty, and settle the mind again. Reading the verses is useful when you lose clarity of focus in meditation. At the end of the meditation session, seal the practice by dedicating the merit to the enlightenment of all sentient beings.

You should also continue your practice outside formal meditation sessions. As you go through the day, briefly recall from time to time that there is no self to be found within your body and mind. There is only an appearance of a self, like in a dream or an illusion. When you remember this, the disturbing emotions—such as attachment, anger, and jealousy—naturally subside. If you have a strong emotion arise, go through the steps of analyzing to see if that emotion is the self. When you look for this self and do not find it, the emotion will have no ground to stand on, and it will naturally self-liberate. As the afflictive emotions decrease in this way, suffering also decreases.

THE MIND-ONLY TRADITION

The Buddha taught that there are two types of selflessness: the lack of individual self, and the lack of self-entity in phenomena. All Buddhist traditions assert the selflessness of the individual. However, only the two Mahayana philosophical schools, the Mind-Only (Skt.: *Chittamatra*) and Middle Way (Skt.: *Madhyamaka*) traditions, assert that phenomena lack self-entity—that the nature of all phenomena is emptiness.

From the perspective of conduct, these two Mahayana schools are not very different—they both emphasize the importance of altruistic activity. But from the perspective of view, the Mahayana is divided into the Mind-Only and the Middle Way schools.

According to the Mind-Only school, all dualistic appearances of a perceived object existing separately from its perceiving subject do not truly exist, and genuine reality is empty of this seeming duality. The verses in this section explain why it is that duality is not real; how dualistic appearances are like appearances in dreams; and how to meditate on essential reality free from duality.

APPEARANCES ARE MIND-ONLY BECAUSE DIFFERENT BEINGS PERCEIVE DIFFERENT APPEARANCES

Looking at the same river,
Humans and fish see it differently.
Similarly, for the six types of beings, there are five ways of seeing.
Therefore, all appearances are the confused projections of
     habitual tendencies. (9)

The only way we are able to know an external object is through our perception of it. If a single object is perceived in different ways by different beings, which of these perceptions is an accurate reflection of the object itself? For example, when a person and a fish look at the same river, they see it in two different ways. Being humans, we do not need an explanation for the way we see water. However, animals such as fish see it differently from humans: they see water as their home. Both humans and fish see the river plainly and clearly with direct valid cognition, yet when they look at it, they see different things.

While there is a limitless, immeasurable, inconceivable number of beings wandering in samsara, if you group all beings into similar kinds, they fall into six classes—gods, demigods, humans, animals, hungry ghosts, and hell beings. All are called "wanderers" because they migrate ceaselessly from one samsaric existence to the next under the power of their confused projections of duality, which they take to be truly existent, causing them to perform confused karmic actions. For as long as they think dualistic appearances exist, they have no power to prevent themselves from wandering in samsara and suffering along the way.

These six types of sentient beings see things in five different ways (the way demigods see things is not explained to be different from the gods'). For example, when looking at water, gods and demigods see delicious nectar; hungry ghosts see blood and pus; and beings in the hell realms see molten lava. All these different modes of perception are asserted to be the confused projections of habitual tendencies. The confusion is that sentient beings think that what they perceive truly exists externally, but it does not. So the confusion is not in the appearance itself but in how we think about it; thinking it truly exists is a mistake, a confused notion.

You may wonder, "Even though this object, what we humans call 'water,' is seen in different ways by different beings, is there still some externally existent object which is being interpreted in these various ways?" There is not, because there are no truly existent particles of matter constituting the object. This will be explained further in verse eleven, "All Happiness and Suffering Is Mind-Only."

Since beginningless time, we sentient beings have developed habitual patterns of perception. Each sentient being's patterns are different, but each sentient being believes that what their habitual projections cause them to perceive truly exist as outer objects. By doing this lifetime after lifetime, we develop strong concepts that objects exist in the way that they appear. However, outer objects do not exist as we think they do, because if an external object actually existed in its own right, then all beings would see it in the same way. Since different sentient beings see things differently, the Mind-Only school asserts the lack of true existence of external objects.

THE BODY IS A CONFUSED APPEARANCE

Since the different ways my body is seen
By enemies, friends, insects, tigers, leopards, and others
Are all established by their own direct perception,
My body is a confused appearance arising due to habitual
    tendencies. (10)

This verse points out that since the body is perceived in different ways by different beings, the body is therefore only a confused appearance and does not truly exist.

Some beings perceive my body as that of an enemy. Viewing my body in this hostile way, when they see it, they feel repulsed. Others perceive it as the body of a friend; such an amicable view of it is characterized by finding it pleasant to see. These are the ways enemies and friends see things. So, even within the range of humans, this body is perceived differently by different people.

There are further variations in the perception of this body for other classes of beings. Tigers, leopards, and insects eat the body's flesh and drink its blood, so they see it as food. Most of us have no experience of being eaten by tigers or leopards, but we have vivid experiences of insects eating our flesh and drinking our blood, so insects are included in this verse as something to which we can all relate.

These different ways sentient beings see my body are not merely the results of their own inferences or surmising, they are different direct perceptions. For example, when someone looks at my body as an enemy, they directly experience repulsion and disgust. However, if a friend looks at me, they have a pleasant feeling, and that too is a direct experience. Therefore, however the body appears, it is a confused appearance arising from individual sentient beings' different habits of perception. In exactly the same way, all appearances are the confused projections of habitual tendencies.

This verse can be presented in terms of a logical reasoning. A logical reasoning consists of: a subject about which an assertion is made; a quality that is asserted or denied with regard to that subject; and a reason that proves the subject has or does not have that quality. In this verse, the subject is "my body"; the quality is being "a confused appearance arising due to habitual tendencies"; and the supporting reason is the "different ways my body is seen by enemies, friends, insects, tigers, leopards, and others are all established by their own direct perception." To put it all together: My body is a confused appearance arising from habitual tendencies, because it is perceived directly in different ways by different beings.

My body could be food and drink for mosquitoes and, since that would benefit them, that would be good and they should drink from my body. There are so many little insects that we cannot avoid harming or killing some of them as we go around, but we cán benefit mosquitoes. The nineteenth-century Tibetan master Paltrul Rinpoche and his students had a tradition of offering their flesh and blood to mosquitoes and other insects. It is good for us all to make such offerings. And when an insect feeds on your body, make aspiration prayers that it will be reborn as your student when you attain enlightenment. The Buddha did that himself in his lifetimes before attaining enlightenment.

All Happiness and Suffering Is Mind-Only

In a dream, from the body's perspective
There is no difference between being shot with an arrow or
    showered with flowers.
However, from the mind's perspective there is a difference.
Therefore, all happiness and suffering should be known as only
    mind. (11)

Happiness and suffering do not truly exist; they are only mind. This is illustrated by the example of having dreams of your body being shot with an arrow or showered with flowers. From the perspective of the dream body, there is no difference between these two experiences, because the dream arrow, flowers, and body are not made of even the smallest particles of matter. They are mere appearances, appearance-emptiness.

The Mind-Only school explains that, similar to a dream, outer objects in the daytime do not truly exist either, because their tiniest material particles do not truly exist. For if there were a truly existent smallest particle of matter it would have to be partless, because if it had parts it could still be further broken down into smaller particles. But a partless particle cannot logically exist, because even the tiniest particle must have a top part and a bottom part, a left part and a right part; it must have some dimensionality in space. If it did not, it could not join with other particles to make larger entities. Therefore, there is no such thing as a particle that has no parts. Thus, while outer objects appear, they are empty of particles of matter and so they do not truly exist.

To return to the dream example, although there is no true difference between a dream arrow and a dream flower hitting your dream body, from the perspective of the thoughts in your mind that believe the dream is real, there appears to be a big difference. If you are showered with flowers, you will feel happy; if you are shot with an arrow, you will not. At parties in India and Nepal, garlands of flowers are thrown and that makes people happy. If one is shot with an arrow, one will experience fear and pain. In our usual way of thinking, we assume that some external objects cause happiness and others cause suffering. The Mind-Only school shows that those objects do not truly exist outside, and it is only confused habitual thoughts that produce the appearance of these objects and the feelings we experience from seeming to come into contact with them.

Another example is being invited to a feast. If you go to a feast as a guest, you eagerly anticipate it. As you travel toward the venue, you get more excited the closer you get. However, if instead of going to the feast as a guest you go as the food, you will have a different feeling about attending it. As you travel toward the venue, you will become more and more afraid and wonder how you can escape. Both these experiences just happen in the mind. For the body, going to the feast in either of these ways is the same. The difference is only from the perspective of conceptual mind. From the perspective of the object there is no difference, and from the perspective of nonconceptual mind there is no difference. Since the only difference exists for conceptual mind, all happiness and suffering is only mind.

The logical reasoning for this verse is as follows: All happiness and suffering is only mind—the confused projections of mind's habitual tendencies—because while from the perspective of the objects themselves there are no differences, from the perspective of mind that clings to the objects as being truly existent, there are differences. An illustrating example is the dream body being shot with an arrow or showered with flowers.

When you find yourself suffering because of clinging to outer objects as being truly existent, remember that outer objects do not truly exist because they are not made of any particles of matter, like in dreams; and the suffering arising from them is also like a dream. The more certainty you have in this, the more relaxed you will be.

ALL PHENOMENA ARE MIND-ONLY

In a dream, even though object and consciousness are not
    sequential,
We mistakenly believe that the object exists before we perceived it.
Similarly, all objects and consciousnesses arise simultaneously,
Therefore, all phenomena are asserted to be only mind. (12)

In this verse, the fact that all phenomena are only mind is proven by an analysis of the process of perception. You might believe that the external world exists independently of your perception of it. Seemingly, an outer object exists first, and then you come along and perceive it. However, the perceived external object does not actually exist before the consciousness that perceives it—they arise simultaneously. Therefore, outer objects do not truly exist, they are only mind.

For example, when we see the form of a friend or an enemy and think that person's form existed before our perception of it, that is confusion. It is like a dream during which we may think that objects—forms, sounds, smells, tastes, and bodily sensations—exist before the consciousnesses that perceive them, but they do not. In dream perception, the perceived object and the perceiving subject are not sequential, they are simultaneous.

We ordinarily think the outer objects we perceive, like mountains, rivers, and stars, exist before we perceive them. We may even think that they have existed for millions of years before we encountered them, and therefore, they truly exist outside of our perception of them. But that way of thinking is confused, for how could a perceived object exist independently of mind's perception of it? What characteristics would it have? Those characteristics could not be known by the mind, because they would have to exist independent of and separate from mind. Unknowable characteristics could be posited, but never verified or perceived. That is why the only characteristics an object can possibly have are those that the mind can possibly know. Therefore, perceived objects and their characteristics are only mind.

Furthermore, all those characteristics of an object that consciousness perceives exist only at the moment of and together with perception of them. For if a perceived object existed before its perceiving consciousness, what would be perceiving it? What would know it? It would be a perceived object without a perceiving subject, which would be illogical. Similarly, the perceiving subject cannot exist before the object it perceives, because if it did it would be a perceiver without an object of perception. Since the perceived object and the perceiving subject must exist together with each other in this simultaneous way, one does not exist outside or independent of the other—object and subject are both merely mind. For example, when we see a rock mountain in a dream we may assume that it existed there long before we perceived it, but it did not. The appearance of the perceived rock mountain and the perceiving consciousness are precisely simultaneous. The same is true during the day, and therefore, external objects are only mind.

The logical reasoning this verse presents is: All phenomena are only mind, because the perceived object and its perceiving consciousness are neither sequential nor separate, but rather are precisely simultaneous. The illustrating example is a dream wherein the perceived object and perceiving consciousness do not exist sequentially even though they are mistakenly believed to do so.

Enemy and Friend Are Mind-Only

We find our friends pleasant,
But when we get angry, they displease us.
We find enemies unpleasant,

But when they become our friends, they please us.

Therefore, both friends and enemies are also only mind. (13)

Why are friends and enemies only mind? When we meet close friends and family, seeing their forms and hearing their voices make us feel good. However, when we get angry at those friends and relatives, we find them repugnant, and they can even become our enemies. When your best friend becomes your enemy, they become your worst enemy. This is because when you were friends, you talked to them about everything and shared all your secrets. When they become your enemy, they know so much about you that it is horrifying.

The opposite can also happen: Your enemy, whose form and voice you once found repugnant, can become your friend, whom you now very much enjoy seeing and speaking with. And your worst enemy can even become your best friend because when they were your worst enemy, you only went around saying bad things about them; but now, you cannot say bad things about them anymore, you have nothing like that left to say, so you speak only of their good qualities.

Thus, both classifications of enemy and friend are only mind, because people are not friends or enemies from their own side. Rather, it is only the mind that designates people as enemy or friend, and that designation can change. So neither enemy nor friend truly exists externally; those labels depend on the mind.

The logical reasoning for this verse is: Friend and enemy are only mind, because friends please us, but when we get angry at them, they become enemies who displease us; and enemies displease us, but when they become our friends, they please us.

The Mahayana and Vajrayana teach that friends and enemies are equality; meaning that friends' and enemies' true nature is the same. We need to meditate on friends' and enemies' equality, because both "friend" and "enemy" are the confused projections of habitual tendencies, and by meditating on them as equality, such confused tendencies are purified. Not only should we meditate on friend and enemy being equal, we should also cultivate compassion for friends and enemies alike. That is how to transform our biased compassion and extend it in an unbiased way. That is much easier to do once we understand that friends' and enemies' true nature is equality, and this is one example of how wisdom and compassion complement each other in the Mahayana and Vajrayana.

Meditating on the equality of friends and enemies benefits us in our daily lives, because we suffer greatly from thinking friends and enemies are unequal and from being attached to our friends and angry at our enemies. By meditating on equality, we can lessen such attachment and anger, be happier and more relaxed as a result, and develop compassion that encompasses all beings.

The Cause of Happiness Is Only the Mind

Material enjoyments are renowned as the cause of happiness,
However, those who are free of attachment, like the Lord of
    Yogis, Milarepa,
Are happy even without material possessions.
Therefore, the cause of happiness is just the mind. (14)

The primary material enjoyment is wealth, and a widely held worldly view is that wealth is a cause of happiness. However, there is another perspective: Siddhas, who have realized the true nature of reality, are free of attachment and do not fixate on sensory enjoyments, so even if they have no conveniences and wealth, they are still happy. Therefore, the cause of happiness is also asserted to be just the mind. Not only that, but the external objects that are ordinarily believed to be the causes of happiness do not even truly exist.

From among the many heroic siddhas of Tibet, the land of snows, the greatest was the Lord of Yogis, Milarepa. He spent a long time living in mountain caves singing many songs of great happiness, such as *The Five Kinds of Yogic Joy, The Twelve Kinds of Yogic Joy, The Eighteen Kinds of Yogic Joy,* and *The Thirty-three Kinds of Yogic Joy.* Milarepa's happiness arose precisely because he had no worldly possessions. It is unlikely that a mountain cave would be a comfortable residence for someone with many possessions. They would be afraid of their property being damaged or of robbers coming to steal it; it would be a difficult place for them to stay. But Milarepa was happy not to have worldly possessions. Once, when he was staying in a mountain cave, a robber came in during the night. The robber wondered if he might find some desirable objects to steal, but there were no lights in the cave, so he was just groping around in the dark. Out of the darkness, he heard Milarepa's voice say to him, "I cannot find anything in this cave in the daylight, but you try and see if you can find something in it in the dark of the night." Milarepa laughed heartily, and then even the robber laughed too.

Milarepa was not afraid of losing anything; he had nothing to protect. This is the happiness of not having any possessions. Most of Milarepa's students (including Rechungma, Sahle Ö, and Palderbum, three of his four foremost female disciples) also practiced Dharma in caves, and they were very happy too. They were able to stay happily alone in retreat, because their happiness was that which comes when you do not have any material possessions.

The Suffering of the Lower Realms Is Mind-Only

Since the hell of molten metal and other terrible environs
Were taught to be confused appearances arising from habitual
  tendencies,
Gain certainty that the suffering
Of the three lower realms is only mind. (15)

In *Entering the Bodhisattvas' Way*, the bodhisattva Shantideva describes how the Buddha taught that the molten metal and other torturous environs of the hell realms are not truly existent; they are all just confused appearances arising from the habitual tendencies present in a negative and malicious mind. It is important to gain certainty that all suffering is similarly only mind. To put this verse in the form of a logical reasoning that will help make this vital point clear: The hell of molten metal and all the rest of the lower realms' miseries arise from mind only, because they are confused appearances arising from habitual tendencies. We could also formulate it as follows: The lower realms' suffering is the confused appearance for a malicious and negative mind, so it is nothing other than mind.

The best example for this is a dream. If you dream of being burned by fire, apart from the suffering of being burned by fire that is a confused appearance in your own mind, there is no fire that actually exists—the fire that appears is not made of the tiniest particle of matter. Since there are no particles of fire, there is nothing there that is hot and burning, the defining characteristics of fire. Yet, even though there are no particles of fire, a hot and burning fire appears. Therefore, that fire along with the suffering you experience from being burned by it are just your own confused thoughts.

You should contemplate this example of fire burning in a dream in order to gain certainty that the hell realm of molten metal and all the rest of the lower realms' suffering do not truly exist, but are merely confused appearances. We cannot expect to gain certainty in this immediately or easily, because since beginningless time we have developed the strong habit of clinging to the confused appearances of outer objects as being real. That is why we need to contemplate these teachings well, gain certainty in them, and recall that certainty again and again.

When contemplating, it is important to examine your own experience. By doing so, I think you will understand well how it is that our suffering is just a confused projection of our own thoughts. When we look at our own experience, we see how suffering can arise due to things that do not exist. For example, when we are thirty, forty, or fifty years old, if we dwell on the difficulties we will have to bear when we become eighty or ninety—our physical strength diminishing, being alone, and lacking resources—then we begin to suffer in the present. The conditions for this suffering are still in the future, they do not exist now; yet we still suffer from these nonexistent things. This suffering is therefore clearly created by our own thoughts. It is important to understand well how it is that thoughts produce suffering, for then we can work with our minds in order to reduce suffering. We can gain certainty that the causes of suffering do not truly exist, and when we do, we naturally relax.

THE CELESTIAL GOD REALM IS A CONFUSED APPEARANCE FOR VIRTUOUS MIND

The beautiful sapphire ground
And the multi-jeweled palaces
Of the celestial god realm
Are the confused appearances produced by virtuous mind. (16)

Like suffering, samsara's happiness is also a confused appearance in the mind. It is the confused appearance that results from the actions of a virtuous mind.

The higher realms, whose appearances are produced by positive deeds, are the three realms of gods, humans, and demigods. From among those, the god realm has the greatest opulence. The god realm's sapphire ground and its celestial palaces made of silver, gold, and diamonds are extremely lovely, but they are still confused appearances—the confused appearances for a virtuous mind. A mind that is positive and altruistic produces appearances that are good and pleasing. Therefore, it is better if we practice virtue. However, if we cling to the good appearances that virtuous actions produce as being truly existent, that produces attachment and suffering. That is why it is important to know that even good appearances are only mind.

We might wonder, "If everything is confused appearance, is it acceptable not to perform virtuous activity?" That is not a good way to think, especially as beginners. Such thinking confuses relative reality and genuine reality. In genuine reality, suffering and happiness do not truly exist. In relative reality, they are both confused appearances of mind, one of a nonvirtuous mind and one of a virtuous mind. Nevertheless, it is certain that if we perform positive, altruistic actions, that will produce good appearances, whereas performing negative, malicious actions will produce unpleasant appearances. Initially, we have to perform virtuous actions and refrain from negative actions in order to accumulate sufficient merit to encounter the Dharma teachings and follow the path of Dharma. We should act in accord with the ten types of virtuous action taught by the Buddha:

three associated with the body (not killing, not stealing, and refraining from sexual misconduct); four associated with speech (not lying, not using harsh speech, not slandering, and not gossiping); and three associated with mind (no jealousy, no maliciousness, and not holding mistaken views).

On the other hand, if we think that since everything is confused appearance we can act negatively and it will not make a difference, we will experience the suffering that arises from such actions. We will wander forever in samsara and never free ourselves from suffering. Suffering and happiness exist in exactly the same way, as mere appearances of a confused mind, but until we have realized this, we will experience suffering and happiness as distinct. That is why it is better for us to abandon the causes of suffering in favor of the causes of happiness.

These stages of meditation on emptiness, on genuine reality, are the antidote to confused appearances. Meditating on these stages cuts through the root of samsara, the root of confused appearances. When meditating on genuine reality, one does not conceptualize about virtuous or nonvirtuous actions, or happiness and suffering— one meditates on the true nature that transcends all these extremes.

However, in the postmeditation phase, one practices virtue and abandons nonvirtue; one cultivates an altruistic mind and abandons maliciousness. One does this while reflecting on how all these appearances are appearance-emptiness, like dreams and illusions. That way of practicing virtue and abandoning nonvirtue is excellent, because it combines virtuous actions with wisdom realizing the true nature of reality.

In Mind-Only, Meditate on Dharmata Empty of Duality

According to the Mind-Only school,
Dualistic appearances are confused,
And Dharmata empty of duality is genuine reality.
Therefore, meditate on Dharmata empty of duality. (17)

This verse explains why we should meditate according to the Mind-Only view as presented in the previous verses. According to the Mind-Only school, the dualistic appearances of perceived objects and perceiving subjects are confused appearances of relative reality. Dharmata, free from the duality of perceived and perceiver, is genuine reality. Therefore, we should meditate on Dharmata empty of duality, because that is the remedy for clinging to the confused appearances of duality as being truly existent.

THE WAY TO MEDITATE

Since perceived objects are the confused projections of habitual
    tendencies, they do not truly exist.
Therefore, the mind that perceives them does not truly exist either.
When you gain certainty that reality is empty of this duality,
Settle naturally into that—without contrivance, let go and relax. (18)

When meditating on the view of the Mind-Only school, first gain certainty that outer objects do not truly exist; they are just confused appearances arising from habitual tendencies, as in dreams. Since there is no perceived outer object, there is no perceiving inner subject either. Therefore, genuine reality is empty of the duality of perceived and perceiver. When you have certainty that there is no such duality, settle naturally into that without thinking or contriving anything else. Let go and relax right within that certainty in nonduality.

If you recite these verses again and again, and contemplate them again and again, you will gain certainty in their profound meaning. Certainty does not arise by thinking, "It is like this." That is just a mere opinion and does not help much. Certainty arises through repeated contemplation. If you do not have certainty, that simply shows that you need to recite the verses and contemplate them more.

When you meditate, recite the verses to refresh the certainty in your mind. Then rest in the certainty that essential reality (Dharmata) is free from the duality of perceived object and perceiving subject. In between your meditation sessions, periodically remind yourself that the appearances of duality you perceive are like a dream.

The Middle Way Empty-of-Self Tradition

In the Middle Way there are two traditions, Empty-of-Self* and Empty-of-Other.** The Middle Way Empty-of-Self tradition is based on *The Transcendent Wisdom Sutras* of the second turning of the wheel of Dharma, further clarified by such texts as Nagarjuna's *Collections of Reasonings*.***

All Phenomena Are Empty of Essence

All phenomena are empty of essence,
Their appearance is the convergence of dependently arisen
    causes and conditions.
Fixating on appearances as truly existent is only confused
    thought,
Like being burned by fire in a dream. (19)

The Middle Way Empty-of-Self tradition refutes all possible kinds of true existence. Thus outer and inner appearances, all the phenomena that make up samsara and nirvana, are empty of essence. "Empty of essence" means not truly existent, naturally empty.

Phenomena being naturally empty means that their basic nature is emptiness. It is not that initially phenomena existed and later they became empty; rather, phenomena have been empty from the very beginning. Whatever phenomenon it is, it has no essence from the start. It is like in a dream where appearances are not real from the first moment they are perceived. All these terms—empty of essence, naturally empty, not truly existent—have the same meaning.

Although in genuine reality phenomena are empty of essence, in relative reality they appear due to causes and conditions. For example, when a flower arises, that flower needs a seed to be its cause, and

* Tibetan: *rang-tong*.
** Tibetan: *shen-tong*.
*** The six texts that constitute Nagarjuna's *Collections of Reasonings* are: *The Fundamental Wisdom of the Middle Way, The Precious Garland, The Refutation of Criticism, The Finely Woven, The Sixty Stanzas of Reasoning,* and *The Seventy Stanzas on Emptiness.*

it needs water, fertilizer, heat, moisture, and space to be its contributing conditions. When the cause and the contributing conditions all converge, a particular phenomenon is produced that accords with those causes and conditions. If the seed lacks one condition, such as sunlight, even with all the other conditions in place, it will not grow into a flower. So the result of a flower is dependent on the causes and conditions for a flower coming together.

Furthermore, all these causes and conditions themselves are merely dependently arisen and do not truly exist, because they arise from their own causes and conditions. Appearances that arise in dependence on the coming together of causes and conditions are mere appearances, like appearances in a dream.

Although all outer and inner phenomena are mere appearances, we still cling to them as being real. When we think that things truly exist in the way that they appear, that is just a confused way of thinking. It is like when we dream and we think that what we experience truly exists in the way it appears—those thoughts that cling to true existence are mistaken. In a dream we may think that external objects exist, but they do not actually have the slightest existence at all. In a dream, we may be burned by fire or carried away by a torrent of water—there is the experience of fire or water, but those objects do not truly exist. Similarly, for us right now, in the daytime, it seems that there are a lot of truly existent things. However, beyond the perspective of confused thoughts, these things are not real.

The Reasoning of Neither One nor Many

Without "one," there is no "many,"
And without "many," there is no "one."
Because these are dependently existent
They are asserted to be mere appearances. (20)

One important reasoning the Middle Way uses to prove that phenomena do not truly exist is known as "neither one nor many" and is taught extensively by Shantarakshita in *The Ornament of the Middle Way*. This reasoning begins by noting that whatever phenomenon it is, if it truly exists, it must be either one thing or many things. However, since "one" and "many" themselves are only dependently existent, not only do the concepts of one and many not truly exist, neither does any phenomenon at all.

In general, all phenomena exist dependently and, therefore, they are dependently arisen mere appearances that do not truly exist. Specifically, let us see how that is with the phenomena of "one" and "many." In order to establish "many," first there has to be "one" to be gathered together with other single entities in order to make a multiplicity. Conversely, if there is not "many" in the first place, then "one" cannot exist, because without the concept of plurality there can be no distinct concept of singularity. Therefore, one and many exist only in mutual dependence, and so they have no true existence, no self-nature—they do not exist in and of themselves. It is like a dream: One and many may appear, but since they depend upon each other for their existence, they do not have any essence of their own.

Since one and many are dependently existent, all outer and inner phenomena, all the phenomena of samsara and nirvana, are also dependently existent, dependently arisen mere appearances, because all phenomena have to be either one or many. Lord Nagarjuna explains it in this way (in verse 7 of *The Seventy Stanzas on Emptiness*):

Without "one" there is no "many."
Without "many," there is no "one."
Therefore, dependently arisen things
Have no attributes.

Confused concepts believe that things truly possess attributes such as "clean," "dirty," "pure," "impure," "good," and "bad." However, since one and many are dependently existent, phenomena do not truly exist, and neither do their attributes. Attributes are of the nature of emptiness.

Because all phenomena are neither one nor many, the Middle Way Empty-of-Self tradition explains that the appearances of this life do not truly exist but are dependently arisen, the mere convergence

of causes and conditions, like dreams and illusions. Reflect again and
again on how appearances are like dreams and illusions, and stable
certainty will arise within you.

Stable certainty in the illusory and dreamlike nature of phenomena is important. To help yourself gain certainty, you can recite verses
like the following:

> My eyes see a form,
> But my mind knows it is like a dream.
> My ears hear a sound,
> But my mind knows it is like a dream.

You should make up verses like this for the other sense consciousnesses—the ear-, nose-, tongue-, and body-sense-consciousnesses.
Reciting such verses will help you to remember the true nature of all
your experiences, pleasant and unpleasant. When you can do that,
then whatever appears, you will be open, spacious, and relaxed.

CLINGING TO TRUE EXISTENCE CAUSES SUFFERING TO INCREASE

Even though all phenomena are unborn,
Beings are born again and again in samsara—
This is a mere dependent appearance, the convergence of causes
    and conditions;
When we believe it is real, suffering increases. (21)

The Middle Way teaches that all outer and inner phenomena do not
actually arise. The protector Nagarjuna's *Fundamental Wisdom of the
Middle Way*, the glorious Chandrakirti's *Entering the Middle Way*, and
the bodhisattva Shantideva's *Entering the Bodhisattvas' Way* all teach
how there is no arising. However, in relative reality we perceive arising. This arising is exactly like a dream. In a dream, arising occurs only
from the perspective of confusion; really nothing is arising at all.

It is the same with sentient beings—since beginningless time, they
have seemingly been born over and over again in samsara. At the

same time, this serial rebirth does not actually exist but is a mere dependent appearance, the convergence of causes and conditions. It is comparable to birth in a dream, or an illusion, and we should contemplate this well.

Although sentient beings' birth, life, and death are dependently arisen mere appearances, when one believes they truly exist, one's suffering increases. This is the work of confused thoughts. Initially, thoughts cling to appearances as truly existent, which causes suffering. Then thoughts cling to that suffering itself as truly existent, and this makes suffering grow greater and greater. If you reflect on your own experience, you will see how the more you cling to things as being truly existent, the more you suffer. It is also helpful to contemplate the example of a dream when you do not know you are dreaming. When we dream and do not know it, we take our self and all the sense objects we experience to be truly existent.

Consider as well how it is that believing an enemy truly exists causes you to suffer. How does someone become your enemy? First, they do something harmful to you, and you think that harm truly exists. That makes you think of that person as your enemy and that this enemy truly exists. That causes anger to arise. Due to that anger, your suffering increases. No one who is angry has peace. When we are angry, our bodies become uncomfortably hot and tense, we cannot sleep at night, and we cannot eat or function well during the day—the suffering just keeps building.

However, male and female bodhisattvas with wisdom and compassion are not harmed by enemies. With their wisdom, bodhisattvas see that neither they themselves nor their enemies truly exist; they know that self and other are like dreams and illusions. And with their all-embracing compassion for friends and enemies alike, they do not have the suffering of anger. So bodhisattvas cannot be harmed by enemies; in fact enemies cause the bodhisattvas' accumulation of merit to increase. For us as well, enemies are great friends who help us on the path of Dharma, because when we have patience with enemies we accumulate merit. We develop gratitude to those enemies for helping us work with our minds and progress on the path to liberation.

It is important to examine phenomena like birth and death, and friends and enemies, and understand that they are mere appearances arisen in dependence upon causes and conditions. Then we will not cling to them as truly existent and we will develop the compassion and wisdom of the bodhisattvas. Here is a verse to help you do that:

> We are not truly born
> And yet, there are continual appearances of birth,
> Dependently arisen mere appearances,
> Like birth in a dream.

As in a Dream, It Is Our Own Confusion That Binds Us

> The abiding nature is neither bound nor liberated, and yet
> Sentient beings are bound by karma, kleshas, and suffering.
> But it is our own confusion that binds us,
> Like being bound by confusion in a dream. (22)

In the abiding nature, there is neither bondage nor liberation. Genuine reality is neither bound nor liberated; it is beyond being bound or liberated. Why is this so? Because in genuine reality, there is no truly existent self to be bound, so there is no bondage; and since there is no bondage, there is no liberation either. Furthermore, these contradictory concepts of bondage and liberation do not truly exist because they are mutually dependent. The three *Transcendent Wisdom Sutras*—the greater, middle, and concise versions—teach extensively on how genuine reality is beyond bondage and liberation, and Lord Nagarjuna's *Fundamental Wisdom of the Middle Way* devotes one whole chapter to explaining this as well.*

You might wonder, "Sentient beings perform a variety of karmic actions that cause them to be reborn in samsara. They suffer in a variety of ways. All of these karmic actions, *kleshas* (disturbing emotions),

---

* Khenpo Tsültrim Gyamtso, *The Sun of Wisdom* (Boston: Shambhala Publications, 2003), pp. 99–108.

and experiences of suffering keep sentient beings bound and captive. What about this bondage?"

All of that bondage is just one's own mental confusion binding oneself. Other than one's own confusion there is no captor, for no external captor truly exists. So in genuine reality, captor and captive are nondual, and in apparent reality, it is only we ourselves who hold ourselves captive with our thoughts that believe inner and outer phenomena are truly existent.

This is good news! Since we are the ones that hold ourselves captive, we are the ones with the power to free ourselves. We are like people bound by ropes or iron fetters in a dream when we do not know we are dreaming. Apart from our own thoughts that believe the bondage to be truly existent, there is nothing binding us at all. And if we can recognize that we are dreaming, we will realize that even though bondage appears, there really is no bondage at all. The bondage is self-liberated.

To put this in verse:

All bondage is our own thoughts,
All liberation is our thoughts self-liberated,
So cultivate the wisdom of listening, reflecting, and meditating,
For that is the only way to freedom.

Since the essential nature of thoughts is that they are self-liberated, free in their own place, we must seek our liberation in our own thoughts' essential nature. When we realize the true nature of thoughts, we gain liberation from our thoughts' confusion, the only thing that binds us. Therefore, the method that produces liberation from bondage does not come from the outside; it is the wisdom of listening, reflecting, and meditating. There is no other method for liberation. By listening to or reading about the stages of view, reflecting on their meaning until we understand and have certainty in them, and resting the mind in that certainty, we gain liberation. When we realize that bondage and liberation do not truly exist, we are liberated from the duality of bondage and liberation.

REALIZING DHARMATA FREE OF CONFUSION

In the natural state there is neither permanence nor extinction;
Permanence and extinction are merely conceptual imputations.
When the confusion of conceptual imputation dissolves,
That is the realization of authentic reality free of fabrications. (23)

How can we see the true nature of reality, free from conceptual fab-rications? We must realize that in the natural state, in genuine reality, there are no conceptual fabrications such as permanence or extinc-tion. Therefore, all the inferior views based on concepts of perma-nence and extinction do not truly exist.

Since permanence and extinction do not exist in genuine reality, where do they come from? Let us explore this further. Permanence and extinction are merely conceptual imputations attributed by thoughts. The subtle definition of the view of permanence is *thinking* that something exists. The subtle definition of the view of extinction is *thinking* that something does not exist.* So permanence and ex-tinction are just produced by thoughts, and apart from being merely thoughts' fabrications, they do not exist in the true nature of reality.

In fact, all phenomena are merely conceptual fabrications, concep-tual imputations. Therefore, all of our inferior views and doubts are also merely conceptual imputations and do not truly exist. When all of these confused conceptual imputations dissolve, there is nothing more you have to do. To gain realization, there is no place you have to go to: When conceptual fabrications dissolve, that is realization. There is no realization apart from that. This is because what is to be realized is essential reality free of conceptual fabrications. So when conceptual fabrications dissolve, inconceivable reality is realized. And, although it is called "essential reality beyond concepts," this essential reality does not truly exist either. There really is nothing to realize.

This is important to recall in our meditation practice. We do not

---

* The basic definition of the view of permanence is thinking that something that is impermanent is permanent. The basic definition for the view of extinction is thinking that something goes out of existence when in fact it continues.

have to struggle with our thoughts. As we develop certainty that whatever thoughts we have do not truly exist, we recognize that we do not need to judge our thoughts or be afraid of certain thoughts disturbing our practice. When a thought arises, we can welcome it as a friend of our meditation, and let it naturally and gradually dissolve in its own place. In fact, there was nothing truly there in the first place. To put this into verse:

> Through the power of habitual tendencies, doubts arise;
> Those doubts are merely one's own conceptual imputations.
> When the conceptual imputations of confused mind dissolve,
> Doubts and mistaken views are not abandoned, but self-liberate.

The Middle Way Autonomy School and Consequence School

The Middle Way Empty-of-Self school is divided into the Autonomy (Skt.: *Svatantrika*) and Consequence (Skt.: *Prasangika*) schools. The Autonomy school refutes true existence and asserts that genuine reality is emptiness. The Consequence school is more profound because it refutes true existence and does not assert anything in its place, even emptiness. For the Consequence school, an assertion is a conceptual elaboration and therefore cannot accurately describe the true nature of reality that is inconceivable.

The Way to Meditate in the Autonomy Tradition

Since they are neither one nor many, phenomena have no
   inherent nature.
Since they neither arise, abide, nor cease, thoughts have no
   inherent nature.
Since there is neither bondage nor liberation, the disturbing
   states of mind have no inherent nature.
Knowing this well, rest within great emptiness. (24)

By reading, reciting, and memorizing the previous verses, which give all the reasons why phenomena have no inherent nature, gain certainty

in this. If you are having difficulty with something in particular—
obsessing over an object of your desire or anger; feeling trapped in a
particular situation; trying to make decisions about the future—then
make that object the focus of your analytical meditation. When we
have difficulties, we take the object of that difficulty as truly existent
and this increases our problems. So apply all the reasons that phenomena have no inherent nature to this object and your thoughts
that this object is truly existent.

When you begin to know well that phenomena have no inherent
nature, and that the disturbing states of mind have no inherent nature, then allow the mind to simply rest within great emptiness, vast
and spacious.

The Way to Meditate in the Consequence Tradition

Existent, nonexistent, and so forth,
Empty, not empty, and so forth,
Permanence, extinction, and so forth—
Genuine reality transcends all such conceptual fabrications. (25)

Mind comes up with so many conceptual possibilities to describe
reality, such as existent or nonexistent, empty or not empty, something or nothing. Cut through these concepts and genuine reality is
revealed just as it is—inconceivable and inexpressible. Right within
that, let go and relax.

Between meditation sessions, train in seeing all appearances as
being dependently arisen mere appearances, appearance-emptiness,
like dreams, illusions, water-moons, rainbows, and movies. This is
the practice of "illusion-like samadhi" taught by both the Autonomy
and the Consequence schools.

The Great Middle Way Empty-of-Other Tradition

The essence, buddha nature,
Is empty of adventitious stains

And empty of the fabrications of existence and nonexistence,
Therefore, it is known as "empty-of-other." (26)

"Empty-of-Other" refers to the mode of emptiness of the true nature
of mind, which is also called luminous clarity, the buddha nature, the
intrinsic essence, and the inherent nature. The way the true nature of
mind is empty is that it is not empty of itself, but rather, it is empty of
the adventitious stains of confusion and of the fabrications of existence and nonexistence. It is empty of all these things that it is not; it
is empty of all that is "other" than it. In the Great Middle Way Empty-
of-Other tradition, this empty nature is spoken of using affirmative
language and terms such as buddha nature and luminous clarity.

This may seem to contradict the Empty-of-Self tradition's nega-
tions of any inherent nature or essence in phenomena. In fact, however, there is no contradiction, because all the terms used by the
Empty-of-Other tradition are merely conventional expressions describing the buddha nature, which in genuine reality is beyond existence and nonexistence. The buddha nature's existence is only posited
conventionally. So, in this verse, when it says, "empty-of-other," that
is merely an expression. It is a term used to communicate. Such terms
themselves are not ultimate reality—they are conventional assertions, but the nature to which they refer is the ultimate.

While this buddha nature, this original abiding nature, this actual
intrinsic nature, is not truly existent, neither is it nonexistent; it is not
both of these extremes nor is it neither of them. The buddha nature is
beyond the fabrications of any extreme. It is beyond either extreme of
permanence or extinction; it is empty of the fabrications of existence
and nonexistence. The buddha nature is also originally free of any im-
perfection or flaw. Therefore, whatever mental obscurations or disturbing emotions may appear, they are merely adventitious and temporary.
They do not exist in the true nature of mind. Because the abiding nature
is empty of these fabrications and stains, it is known as Empty-of-Other.

The question then arises: This buddha nature is explained to be
empty of adventitious stains and fabrications, which are all other

than it, but does that mean that it is not empty of its own essence? Ultimately, its essence is beyond all the fabrications of being empty and not empty. In relative reality, which uses conventional terms and designations, it is explained that it is not empty of its own essence, because all the Dharmakaya's qualities, such as luminous clarity, awareness, and bliss, are spontaneously present within it.

There are two Empty-of-Other traditions: Sutra and Secret Mantra Vajrayana. From among the many texts in the Sutra Empty-of-Other tradition, the main one is *The Commentary on the Highest Teachings in the Mahayana Continuum* (Skt.: *Uttara-tantra-shastra*), otherwise known as *The Treatise on Buddha Nature* by Maitreya. This text explains the seven vajra points, the fourth of which is "the element," referring to the buddha nature, the basic element of which mind is made.* Maitreya teaches about the buddha nature in a concise way by means of presenting the three reasons why all beings have the buddha nature; in an extensive way by means of describing the buddha nature's ten aspects; and, finally, by means of nine examples for how the true nature of a sentient being's mind is enlightened while at the same time covered by adventitious stains.

One such example compares the buddha nature to a buddha statue hidden within a decaying lotus blossom. This flawless buddha statue represents the unsullied true nature of mind, luminosity-emptiness inseparable, which is the nature of mind not just of the buddhas and bodhisattvas but of all sentient beings.** The difference between buddhas, bodhisattvas, and ordinary beings, then, is the degree to which this true nature is obscured by the temporary stains of confusion. Ordinary sentient beings have minds whose true nature is obscured by confusion, bodhisattvas have partially purified these obscurations, and the buddhas have completely purified them. All the stages of the path that the Buddha taught have this complete purification as their goal.

* The seven vajra points are the Buddha, the Dharma, the Sangha, the element, enlightenment, qualities, and enlightened activity.
** "Luminosity-emptiness" (or "clarity-emptiness") is actually a way to describe mind's true nature as the union of the luminosity emphasized by the Empty-of-Other school and the emptiness taught by the Empty-of-Self school. For more explanation, see pages 112–14.

While this buddha nature abides within all beings, most of us are unaware of it. We do not realize that what looks so ordinary or even unappealing on the outside—our samsaric condition—holds this precious treasure that can fulfill all our wishes—enlightened mind.

The Treatise on Buddha Nature has been translated into English, German, Chinese, and many other languages, and it excellently presents the view of the Sutra Empty-of-Other tradition. It would be good for you to study it in detail.

The texts on the Secret Mantra Empty-of-Other tradition are the Highest Yoga (Skt.: *Anuttara*) tantras, in particular *The Wheel of Time* (Skt.: *Kalachakra*). Kunkhyen Dolpo Sangye, also known as Dolpopa Sherab Gyaltsen, was one of the great exponents of *The Wheel of Time* and wrote *Mountain Retreat Teachings: The Ocean of Definitive Meaning*, a text on the Empty-of-Other view that quotes from *The Treatise on Buddha Nature* and *The Wheel of Time,* as well as various other texts including *Reciting the Names of Manjushri.* If you wish to understand the Secret Mantra Empty-of-Other tradition, it is good to study this text by Dolpopa.

Since the Empty-of-Other school explains that the mind's true nature has actually always been free of all fabrications and is perfectly pure, its teachings are similar to those of the Mahamudra and Dzogchen traditions. All these traditions emphasize mind's original purity beyond grasping and rejecting.

THE WAY TO MEDITATE IN THE EMPTY-OF-OTHER TRADITION

When we analyze this mind, we cannot find any essence,
But when we do not analyze, experiences of luminosity are
    unceasing.
Therefore, mind is luminosity and emptiness, primordially
    inseparable,
And this is known as luminous clarity, the buddha nature. (27)

The way to meditate according to the Empty-of-Other teachings is to rest within the true nature of mind, which can be described as luminous clarity free of mental fabrications, or luminosity-emptiness inseparable. Mind is the union of luminosity and emptiness because when we analyze the mind, we find it has no essence, but having analyzed, when we let mind rest, we continually experience luminosity. So analyze to gain certainty that mind has no essence, and then let mind settle within its own nature and relax, without analysis or effort. Various appearances of sights, sounds, smells, tastes, and bodily sensations will continually manifest. These are the experiences of luminosity; do not seek to avoid or block them, but do not grasp at them either. During meditation, do not conceptualize about these appearances or label them as "this" or "that." If the mind does reject, grasp, or otherwise conceptually identify objects, then simply return to the true nature of that rejecting, grasping, or identifying—freedom from fabrications.

During daily life, from time to time take a few moments to look at mind's true nature, luminous clarity beyond concepts, and relax. And remember that outer objects are like appearances in a dream, the energy and play of mind's inherent luminosity.

QUESTIONS AND ANSWERS

Question: If there is no self, why are sentient beings confused? If there is no self, why is there suffering?

Khenpo Tsültrim Gyamtso Rinpoche:

> While ultimately there is no self,
> Relatively, there are confused sentient beings.
> While suffering does not truly exist,
> Relatively, there is the suffering of confusion.
> Therefore, one should rely upon both truths—
> Genuine reality and relative reality.

It is important to distinguish between relative reality and genuine reality. Relative reality is simply how things appear to us. It is the coarse misunderstanding and confused experience of appearances when there has been no investigation into their true nature. From this unanalyzed perspective, confused sentient beings exist.

In contrast, genuine reality is ascertained through analysis. It is a more refined understanding that is reached when we look for the true nature of appearances. For example, initially, we question the validity of our assumption that the self is an existent entity. Then, when we analyze, we cannot find the self. Therefore, we conclude that in genuine reality, confused sentient beings do not exist.

Similarly, in genuine reality there is no suffering, it is empty; but in relative reality, for confused sentient beings, there is suffering. This is comparable to a dream: While the suffering in a dream is not truly existent, when we are confused and unaware that we are dreaming, we suffer. For this reason, both relative reality and genuine reality are taught.

Q: If everything is emptiness and sentient beings do not truly exist, how do male and female bodhisattvas benefit others?

KTGR:

> Although the abiding nature is beyond fabrication,
> And bodhisattvas' concepts of fabricated attributes have
>   dissolved,
> In order to be compassionate toward wanderers who lack such
>   realization,
> Bodhisattvas perform unceasing altruistic activity.

Emptiness does not mean complete nothingness. There are appearances of sentient beings, and these beings experience suffering in relative reality. But the abiding nature of all outer and inner phenomena, of all the phenomena of samsara and nirvana, is emptiness beyond conceptual fabrications. Noble male and female bodhisattvas realize this, so their concepts of fabricated attributes have dissolved, and they transcend suffering. However, wandering beings who do not realize the abiding nature do suffer, and so bodhisattvas have compassion for them. Due to their compassion, bodhisattvas uninterruptedly perform altruistic activity until all wandering beings have gained realization and transcended suffering.

Q: If all phenomena are empty, how do we attain buddhahood?

KTGR:

> Ultimate bodhichitta cuts through the root of existence.
> Relative bodhichitta frees you from the extreme of peace.
> Following the Mahayana path leads to enlightenment
> Which does not abide in either extreme of existence or peace—
> How wonderful!

From among the three vehicles—those of the hearers, the solitary realizers, and the bodhisattvas—the bodhisattva vehicle, the Mahayana, is marvelous, a great wonder.* This is because in the Mahayana, the object of meditation is bodhichitta in both its ultimate and relative forms.

Meditating on ultimate bodhichitta means meditating on emptiness, and by doing so, one cuts the root cause of samsaric existence, the confusion of clinging to true existence. Thus, ultimate bodhichitta frees one from the extreme of samsara.

Cultivating relative bodhichitta means giving rise to the desire to attain buddhahood in order to benefit all sentient beings. The fundamental source of relative bodhichitta is compassion—the wish that sentient beings be free from suffering. Therefore, cultivating compassion and relative bodhichitta frees one from the extreme of desiring to obtain nirvanic peace and happiness for oneself alone. In this way, relative bodhichitta frees one from the extreme of nirvana.

---

* The vehicles of the hearers and solitary realizers are the two whose practices are based on the Buddha's teachings in the first turning of the wheel of Dharma. The vehicle of the hearers derives its name from the quality of how intently its followers listen to the Buddha's teachings. The fruition of this vehicle is the attainment of the level of "arhat" (see glossary). The solitary realizers, because of their pride, desire to attain realization by themselves, without a teacher or other students. Thus, in their final lifetime as an ordinary sentient being, they are born in a place where the Buddhist teachings do not otherwise exist. Due to a certain set of circumstances, their past knowledge and habits awaken, and they are able to attain the state of arhat all by themselves, hence their name.

Noble bodhisattvas happily take birth in samsara again and again in order to aid sentient beings.

In this way, relative and ultimate bodhichitta lead to the enlightenment called "non-abiding nirvana" because it does not abide in either extreme of existence or peace, samsara or nirvana. This is why the Mahayana is so marvelous. The Mahayana is a great miracle—the extraordinary vehicle.

Q: If the abiding nature of all phenomena is freedom from fabrications, then why not just say that at the beginning? Why do we have to have all these progressive stages of understanding?

KTGR:

> Our monkey-like thoughts
> Jump between clinging to existence and nonexistence.
> Putting a halt to this clinging is difficult to do all at once,
> So we must give up our clinging step-by-step.

Our fixating thoughts arise in a variety of ways. At times we cling to existence, and at other times to nonexistence. Our clinging is like a monkey: When you try to catch a monkey, it squirms away from you; when you approach it from one direction, it veers off in the opposite direction. Similarly, if we stop our clinging to existence, then we cling to nonexistence. When we stop clinging to nonexistence, then we cling to existence. As we progress on the path, the way we oscillate between these two becomes increasingly subtle. That is why the habitual fixations of thoughts must be approached in stages; trying to purify them all at once is difficult. The abiding nature of all phenomena is freedom from all fabrications, but we cannot dissolve all our fabrications simultaneously.

For this reason, we are taught to approach these thoughts progressively. First, to help us stop clinging to the self as truly existent, we meditate on the stage of the selflessness of the individual. Next, to help us stop clinging to outer objects as truly existent, we meditate within self-awareness empty of perceived and perceiver, as the Mind-Only

tradition instructs. Following that, to help us stop clinging to all phenomena, including self-awareness, as truly existent, we meditate according to the teachings of the Autonomy tradition, which teaches
that all phenomena's true nature is total emptiness like space. Then,
in order to stop clinging to emptiness, we train in the Consequence
school's teachings on the freedom from all fabrications, including
even the fabrication of emptiness. Finally, in order to help ourselves
stop conceptually clinging to freedom from fabrications, we train in
resting in the abiding nature of mind, luminous clarity free of fabrications, as taught by the Empty-of-Other tradition.

Trying to understand all these profound points at once is difficult.
However, when we study and practice them progressively, our mind
gets well-prepared for each subsequent stage, and this makes our
practice go well.

Q: The Mind-Only tradition and the Empty-of-Other tradition both
assert self-awareness. What is the difference between those two
schools' views of self-awareness?

KTGR:

> The Mind-Only tradition's self-awareness
> Is one's own experience of feelings of happiness and suffering.
> The Empty-of-Other tradition's self-awareness
> Is intimately self-aware original wisdom.

According to the Mind-Only school, since the perceived object does
not exist, then neither does the perceiver. The support for this emptiness of the duality of perceived and perceiver is consciousness that is
merely lucid awareness. This nondual self-awareness is the Mind-
Only tradition's explanation of self-awareness.

Sometimes we experience happiness and sometimes suffering.
At other times, various thoughts of desire and anger arise. One is
unable to show mind's feelings and thoughts to other people; these
mental experiences are ultimately inexpressible. Furthermore, it is

not possible for others to have one's own direct experience of one's own mind. One's own feelings of happiness and sorrow and one's own thoughts of desire and anger are one's own private experiences. In the Mind-Only tradition, one's own inexpressible experience of these feelings and thoughts is what is meant by self-awareness. The Mind-Only school believes that this self-awareness is a truly existent entity.

The Great Middle Way Empty-of-Other tradition describes self-awareness as intimately self-aware original wisdom. It is aware of its own essence in a nondual manner, in a way in which there is no duality of an object of awareness and a subject aware of that object. The state of mind that is aware of its intrinsic essence, in which known and knower are nondual, is called self-awareness. This awareness is the abiding nature of one's mind, but it is not a truly existent entity, it is luminosity-emptiness inseparable. Another way to describe it is to say that the self-awareness of the Mind-Only tradition is the self-experience of consciousness; the self-awareness of the Empty-of-Other tradition is the self-experience of wisdom.

The Mind-Only school teaches us that all phenomena are only mind, and the Middle Way explains that all phenomena are emptiness. Both of these explanations help us to stop clinging to appearances as being truly existent.

> Clinging to this life as truly existent
> And clinging to aging, sickness, and death as truly existent
> Occur from the perspective of confused consciousness,
> And not from the perspective of perfect wisdom.

The appearances of this life—all the various appearances of forms, sounds, smells, tastes, and bodily sensations we perceive—seem to truly exist. But life's appearances do not say to us, "I am real." They only seem to be real from our confused thoughts' perspective when we think, "Those things really exist out there." That is like what we do in a dream when we do not know we are dreaming.

Similarly, we mistakenly believe that aging, sickness, and death are truly existent. From among the four basic kinds of suffering— birth, aging, sickness, and death—in this life we have already had the experience of birth and we do not remember it. So we mainly cling to aging, sickness, and death as truly existent, but that is just confused consciousness at work. The buddhas' perfect wisdom does not view this life, or the aging, sickness, and death that occur within it, as truly existent. The noble buddhas and bodhisattvas with wisdom that sees genuine reality do not see these events as real. Training in the view of the Mind-Only school that all phenomena are mind, and in the Middle Way view that all phenomena are emptiness, helps us transform our confused consciousness into perfect wisdom.

CONCLUDING INSTRUCTION

> If you have faith in genuine Dharma, and joyous diligence in its
>   practice,
> Then purify your mindstream with great love and compassion,
> And do not ever be discouraged
> From accomplishing great benefit for all sentient beings, includ-
>   ing your enemies. (28)

When we have faith in genuine Dharma, it is a joy to practice it. Initially, it may feel like an effort to practice the teachings, but gradually we experience their benefit and practice becomes joyful. We feel so lucky to have found these teachings and to be able to practice them.

With this foundation, our ability to increase love and compassion is limitless. Through developing love and compassion we purify all the negativity from our mindstreams that comes from clinging to self.

With the knowledge that any circumstance in which we find ourselves is not truly existent, every situation is workable and provides an opportunity to practice. Consequently, nothing can possibly discourage us. We continually work for the benefit of ourselves and all sentient beings without any bias.

DEDICATION OF MERIT

> By the power of explaining and practicing the stages of medita-
> tion on emptiness, genuine reality,
> Which cut through the root of samsara,
> May I and all limitless sentient beings
> Attain perfect, unsurpassable enlightenment.

There are five stages to this meditation on emptiness—the way to meditate on selflessness; the way to meditate on Dharmata empty of duality in Mind-Only; the way to meditate in the Autonomy tradition; the way to meditate in the Consequence tradition; and the way to meditate in the Empty-of-Other tradition. When you read, contemplate, and meditate on *The Stages of View at the Heart of Definitive Meaning* again and again, its meaning will become clearer and clearer, and this will bring great benefit for yourself and others.

COLOPHON*

This text was spontaneously spoken by the one only called "Khenpo," Tsültrim Gyamtso. May it be auspicious!

* Tibetan compositions traditionally have colophons, and therefore one is found here at the end of *The Stages of View at the Heart of Definitive Meaning*, as well as *A Prayer That These True Words Be Swiftly Fulfilled* and *Auspiciousness That Lights Up the Universe* later in this book. Since *The Seven Ways Things Shine Inside and Out* and *The Eighteen Kinds of Yogic Joy* are selections from the larger compendium of Milarepa's biography and songs, they do not have colophons.

Part Two

Songs of Realization in Dharma Practice

3

Skillful, Enjoyable, Wonderful

Singing as Buddhist Practice

An Overview by Ari Goldfield

THOSE WHO ARE familiar with Khenpo Rinpoche and his teaching style know of his special emphasis on Buddhist songs. In such songs Dharma practitioners can express any aspect of the path, and the songs of the great masters are Rinpoche's focus in that he studies them, memorizes them, explains them to his students, sings them, and has his students sing them too. He has also composed many profound songs himself. In all these ways, Rinpoche has demonstrated to his students what a wonderful Dharma practice singing can be.

The tradition of Buddhist singing goes all the way back to the Buddha Shakyamuni himself. The Buddha's teachings are divided into twelve sections, and one of these is the "Set of Teachings Given in Melody." These were the teachings that the Buddha actually sang to his students.

Then, at the start of the Kagyu lineage that Rinpoche holds, the great masters Tilopa, his student Naropa, and Naropa's student Marpa each sang many songs of realization. And the one who sang the most songs of all was Marpa's student, the Lord of Yogis, Milarepa. Perhaps it is no coincidence that of all the countless Tibetan masters who achieved high levels of realization, the one who sang the most songs, Milarepa, is also the only one who is universally acknowledged by Tibetan Buddhists of all lineages to have attained perfect enlightenment.

Milarepa sang about all aspects of the path of Dharma and how he integrated Dharma practice into his own life. He even sang this verse about singing itself:

> Singing the key instructions
> Isn't meaningless,
> It's the lineage tradition.

WHY SING?

The great masters of the past and present emphasize singing because it is such a skillful method of Dharma practice. The first benefit of singing Dharma teachings is that it is much easier to learn a song by heart than it is to memorize prose. Singing Dharma songs therefore allows us to easily remember the Dharma's essential instructions. That is beneficial because when our minds are agitated by suffering, and especially at the point of death—which could come suddenly and without warning—we want to be able to remember the key points of practice as readily as possible, without having to look them up in a book or else be unclear what to do.

Singing also improves our meditation because it is an excellent remedy for meditation's two main obstacles: dullness and agitation. Mental dullness and fogginess evaporate quickly when we sing in a strong and clear voice. And singing prevents mind from becoming agitated or distracted by outer objects, because mind has the song to hold on to as a stabilizing focus of attention. With dullness and agitation cleared away, we can concentrate well on the meaning of the song we are singing, and our understanding and meditation improve.

Furthermore, singing has a positive effect on the subtle channels and energies in our bodies. At the crown of the head, throat, heart, and navel, many subtle channels come together in what the Vajrayana teachings call "chakras." If the channels in these chakras (particularly the heart chakra) become constricted and energy gets stuck there, we can feel anxious and uncomfortable. Singing in a strong and clear voice opens up the channels, which allows the subtle energies in the body to flow easily, bringing us relaxation and clarity. A person can definitely experience this happening whether or not they have studied the Vajrayana teachings on the subtle body.

Finally, singing is enjoyable. If we like a particular type of Dharma practice we will do it more often, which only brings benefit to ourselves and others. Not everyone enjoys singing right away—some students are initially put off by the singing they encounter at one of Khenpo Rinpoche's teachings. But in so many cases people find that over time they perceive its benefits and enjoy it more and more, until they become some of the most enthusiastic singers of all.

SINGING IN DIFFERENT LANGUAGES AND MELODIES

Khenpo Rinpoche instructs his students to sing translations of Indian and Tibetan Dharma songs in the students' native languages and melodies. Sometimes people ask: "Why are you singing in English and other languages instead of Sanskrit or Tibetan? Should you not sing in those blessed traditional languages of the Dharma?" In fact, to sing in one's own language is the Buddhist tradition. It is taught that one of the miraculous features of the Buddha's speech was that his teachings were understood by all listeners, each in their own individual language. Therefore, the Buddha did not truly speak any one particular language. There is no one language that is inherently more blessed than any other. Certainly, Sanskrit and Tibetan are blessed by the realized masters who practiced in those languages, but just as Tibetans did with their own language when they began practicing Buddhism so many centuries ago, so can modern Dharma practitioners bless their own languages by using them for Dharma practice.

People also inquire about the songs' original melodies, and about the appropriateness of using new ones. Rinpoche states that there is no way to know what the original melodies were. Rinpoche himself has made up melodies, and he also sings melodies his teachers created. He teaches that what is important is to *sing* the songs, which one will do more often if one enjoys the melodies. That is why it is good to sing in melodies that are harmonious with our own cultures.

In fact, singing in culturally familiar melodies is also a tradition that dates back to the time of the Buddha. When the Buddha's monks first started to chant his verses, it is said that the local Indian people thought it sounded awful. No one liked to listen to the monks sing. So the Buddha instructed the monks to sing in melodies that people would like. The monks used the melodies of the Indian Hindu Brahmans, and the people were pleased.*

Milarepa's Inspirational Life, and His Songs in this Book

Over the decades, Khenpo Rinpoche has given so many wonderful teachings on the songs of realization sung by a great variety of realized teachers. And the master whose songs Rinpoche has sung and taught the most is Milarepa.

Milarepa is renowned and revered not only for his attainment of enlightenment, but equally for the way in which he did so. As a child he endured tremendous suffering; as a youth he committed unspeakable deeds of killing and destruction; and as a man he unshakably dedicated himself, in the face of all hardships, to cultivating wisdom and compassion. Whether it was a lack of adequate food or clothing, harsh weather, or harassment by robbers and family enemies—whatever difficulties Milarepa faced, he found sanctuary in the armor of patience, the strength of altruism, and the citadel of the true nature of mind. By doing so he transformed obstacles into epiphanies; enemies into friends and students; suffering into joy; and he became an inspiration over the past nine centuries to countless people who have encountered his story. In times of difficulty Tibetans regularly turn for solace to a book containing Milarepa's biography and songs; some who go to practice retreat in mountain caves carry with them only that book. Even some Chinese Communists came to admire Mi-

---

* Brahmans are the Hindu caste of priests.

larepa—there are accounts of Chinese officials in certain areas telling Tibetans that practicing Dharma by staying in monasteries and accepting offerings from the people was a drain on society's resources and therefore forbidden; however, anyone who wanted to practice Dharma like Milarepa and stay by themselves in a cave would be allowed to do so.

Of all of Milarepa's songs that Rinpoche has taught us (and which we aspire to publish along with Rinpoche's explanations in future volumes), *The Seven Ways Things Shine Inside and Out* is the first one presented here, because in it Milarepa gives us an overview of all the stages of his life and how he applied Dharma practice in each one of them. Then in *The Eighteen Kinds of Yogic Joy*, presented next, Milarepa sings to us of how, as a result of his realization of the true nature of reality, he is able to enjoy all the episodes in his very recognizably human life, complete with its great variety of experiences and emotions, in an equally delightful, spacious, and courageous fashion.

Both of these songs are filled with insights for us, and by reading, contemplating, and singing them, we connect with Milarepa's own experience and realization in a way that edifies and elevates our own.

How to Practice "Singing Meditation"

Khenpo Rinpoche has explained that there are different ways you can meditate while singing. First, you can let your mind rest one-pointedly on the sound of the melody while you sing.* Doing just that is a way to practice *shamatha* (calm-abiding) meditation. And if, while doing that, you let your mind rest right within the sound's true nature, sound-emptiness, that is *vipashyana* (superior insight) meditation. If you let your mind rest in the recognition that the nature of the sound and your mind perceiving it are undifferentiable, that is the Mahamudra meditation called "meditating with appearances."

---

* To sing these songs, you can download the melodies from the *Stars of Wisdom* website, www.starsofwisdom.info. Or, you can make up your own melodies if you like. The important thing is to sing the songs in a way that you enjoy.

You can also focus on the meaning of the words, and in that way practice what is called the "meditation with the focus of the learned ones," because you are learning something at the same time you are meditating. You are learning the profound words of the Dharma and reflecting on their meaning, and so while you meditate your wisdom is increasing.

Finally, you can do the Mahamudra practice called "meditating with the moving mind" by looking directly at the nature of the thoughts that arise while you sing, and relaxing in their essential nature—clarity-emptiness, luminosity, great bliss.

4

The Seven Ways Things Shine Inside and Out

Milarepa's Song of Realization,
with Commentary

TRANSLATED BY ARI GOLDFIELD

MILAREPA'S LIFE STORY is remarkable. When he was young, he suffered a lot and performed terribly negative actions. Then he felt deep regret at how he had been living his life, and he had an intense yearning to gain liberation and attain enlightenment by practicing Dharma. He met his guru, Marpa the King of Translators, and endured all the very difficult trials that Marpa put him through before he would teach Milarepa how to practice. After receiving Marpa's teachings, Milarepa practiced one-pointedly, unwavering in the face of a variety of extremely trying circumstances, and eventually he achieved perfect enlightenment. As a teacher, Milarepa greatly benefited many sentient beings. His example inspires us, and his profound songs teach us how to practice in a way that we can achieve the same results that he did.

In *The Seven Ways Things Shine Inside and Out*, Milarepa sings about the stages of his life in relation to how he progressed on his Dharma path. This is a song that teaches us about connections and interdependence: If we want a good result from our Dharma practice, what conditions do we need to come together externally, internally, and then what do we need to happen as a result "in between"?

The Seven Ways Things Shine Inside and Out

Outside my father and mother were shining
Inside my all-base consciousness shone
And in between, I got this human body complete
I wasn't born in the lower realms—that's all I've got!

Outside the scenes of birth and death are shining
Renunciation and faith shine inside
And in between, I remember true Dharma so divine
Nobody close to me becomes my enemy—that's all I've got!

Outside my father, the lama is shining
While my own knowledge cleans the stains up inside
And in between, confident understanding starts to gleam
I've got no doubts about Dharma—that's all I've got!

Outside the six kinds of beings are shining
Inside compassion for everyone shines
And in between, I remember my meditation experiences
No self-clinging, only compassion—that's all I've got!

Outside the three realms are shining in freedom
Inside the wisdom, self-arisen, shines
And in between is the confidence of realizing basic being
I've got no fear of the true meaning—that's all I've got!

Outside the five sense pleasures are shining
Inside the wisdom, free of clinging, shines
And in between is conduct where everything tastes the same
I am not thinking joy and pain are different things—that's all I am!

Outside creations are shining in ruins
Inside the freedom from hope and fear shines
And in between, I'm not sick with striving or straining, no, no, no!
I am not thinking right and wrong are two different things—that's
   all I am!*

COMMENTARY

THE PRECIOUS HUMAN LIFE

Outside my father and mother were shining
Inside my all-base consciousness shone
And in between, I got this human body complete
I wasn't born in the lower realms—that's all I've got!

"Outside my father and mother were shining." In the Buddhist tradition, bardo (meaning "intermediate state") is the name given to the time between the end of one lifetime and the beginning of the next. When the bardo ends, one takes on a new existence, and the outer conditions that need to come together if that existence is to be in a human body are a human man and woman. This coming together of Milarepa's future father and mother is the condition that happened on the outside enabling Milarepa's birth as a human being in the family called "Mila."

When Milarepa sings about this, he is remembering his father and mother's kindness in providing him with the main condition needed to obtain a precious human life. Our parents have been kind to us in numerous ways, but the best thing they have done for us is to give us this precious human life that we can use to practice the Dharma. Remembering that, we can feel a wonderful sense of gratitude toward our own fathers and mothers, just as Milarepa does as he begins his song.

"Inside my all-base consciousness shone." According to the traditions that assert that each sentient being has eight consciousnesses, the

* This song was translated under the guidance of Khenpo Tsültrim Gyamtso Rinpoche by Ari Goldfield in 1999. The original Tibetan source is *Mi la ras pa'i rnam mgur* (n.p.: mtsho sngon mi rigs dpe skrun khang, 1989), pp. 298–99.

most subtle of the eight is the "all-base" or just "base" consciousness (Skt.: *alaya-vijnana*), the ground or support for all mental activity.

In general, whatever one perceives, thinks, or does makes an imprint in one's base-consciousness. If one has habitual ways of perceiving, thinking about, or doing things, those habits are stored in the base-consciousness and can grow stronger or weaker depending on whether one continues to follow them or not.

Furthermore, when one performs positive, altruistic actions, they make karmic imprints in one's base-consciousness that will ripen as results one will find enjoyable; and when one performs negative, selfish actions, they make karmic imprints in one's base-consciousness that will ripen as suffering. Particularly here, Milarepa is singing about the positive and negative karmic imprints stored in the base-consciousness that produce rebirth in either the higher or lower realms, respectively.* In Milarepa's past lives he performed the positive, altruistic actions necessary to be reborn as a human being; that karma was stored in his base-consciousness; and at the time of his human birth, that karma ripened. So Milarepa has the inner condition of the positive karma he needs in order to obtain a human body. Thus in this second line, Milarepa teaches us about the importance of performing positive actions that will ripen as good results in future lifetimes.

This result is what Milarepa sings about in the third line: "In between, I got this human body complete." "Complete" means that not only is it a human life, but it is a life that can be used to practice Dharma, because it has the necessary three qualities of: faith in the Buddha's teachings; joyous diligence in putting these teachings into practice; and the wisdom necessary to know both how to practice and how to gain awareness of the true nature of reality realized through that practice. These are the three qualities that make one's human existence a precious human existence—the three conditions that allow one to practice the Dharma.

---

* The higher realms are the gods, demigods, and humans; the lower realms are the hells, hungry ghosts, and animals.

Then, when Milarepa sings, "I wasn't born in the lower realms—that's all I've got," he is saying: "I have not got much, but what I have got is that I was not born in one of the hell realms, as a hungry ghost, or as an animal. In past lifetimes I performed positive actions and made aspiration prayers to be able to practice Dharma, so now I have this precious human body that I can use toward that end."

This first verse then is a teaching from the perspective of relative, apparent reality, about the precious human birth, karmic cause and result, and the suffering of samsara. However, it is important to remember that these phenomena are dependently arisen mere appearances, and in genuine reality, they do not truly exist. Their true nature is emptiness.

RENUNCIATION OF SAMSARA AND FAITH IN DHARMA

Outside the scenes of birth and death are shining
Renunciation and faith shine inside
And in between, I remember true Dharma so divine
Nobody close to me becomes my enemy—that's all I've got!

When Milarepa sings "Outside the scenes of birth and death are shining," he is referring first of all to the death of his father, Sherab Gyaltsen. If you have read Milarepa's life story, you will be familiar with how Sherab Gyaltsen died when Milarepa was very young. Sherab Gyaltsen's will left all of his possessions in the care of Milarepa's uncle and aunt as trustees for Milarepa, his mother, Nyangtsa Kargyen, and his sister, Peta. Milarepa's uncle and aunt abused that trust, however, and treated Milarepa's family terribly. Milarepa's uncle and aunt forced his family to be their servants, to live in poverty, and treated them with disrespect and disregard for their well-being. As a result, Milarepa suffered a great deal.

Then, at his mother's command, Milarepa trained in black magic so that he could take revenge on his uncle, aunt, and the villagers who had mistreated his family. Milarepa did this successfully, and used sorcery to kill many people and destroy the villagers' crops. Later, Milarepa felt intense regret for his negative actions, and so he suffered even more.

However, the end result of Milarepa's difficult experiences turned out to be positive. As Milarepa sings in the next line, "Renunciation and faith shine inside." As a result of his suffering, Milarepa came to feel a deep sense of renunciation of samsara and faith in the Dharma.

This is one of the reasons why suffering is a friend of our Dharma practice. The more we suffer, the more we understand that it is impossible to find happiness in outer appearances, which constantly change in ways that are beyond our control. The more we renounce that quest to find happiness on the outside, the more we gain certainty that the way to happiness is to discover it inside of ourselves—in the true nature of our mind, the buddha nature, stainless luminous clarity. The more certainty we have that the Buddha's teachings help us to realize the true nature of mind—the genuine and reliable source of happiness—the more faith we have in the Dharma.

And so Milarepa sings, "And in between, I remember true Dharma so divine." As a result of the outer condition of seeing death happen, and the inner condition of having renunciation and faith arise within himself, Milarepa remembers the true Dharma and how important it is to practice it. The Dharma is called "divine" because it is beneficial—it helps us and others gain freedom from suffering. It is important to remember that Dharma can benefit us so much.

Milarepa does remember this, and as a result he sings: "Nobody close to me becomes my enemy—that's all I've got!" For Milarepa, whatever harm someone might appear to do him, the only way that anyone could be his enemy is if they prevented him from practicing Dharma. So he sings that he does not let any of his close relatives become an obstacle to his practice.

For example, when Milarepa was meditating in the mountains and putting himself through a great number of physical austerities, his sister, Peta, and his former fiancée, Dzeeseh, would come to see him from time to time. In particular, his sister would look at Milarepa's emaciated condition and feel very sad about seeing her brother wasting away up in the mountains. She begged him many times to come down, adopt a normal life, live in a house, and accumulate wealth like everybody else did. But Milarepa did not listen to her—he just continued to practice in the same way as before. So Milarepa did not let Peta and Dzeeseh's entreaties come between him and his Dharma practice, and not only that, eventually both of them became his Dharma students.

Ordinary, worldly enemies cannot really be obstacles to our Dharma practice, because the more harm that anyone does to us, the stronger our renunciation becomes, and the stronger our inspiration to practice the Dharma that leads to liberation. Also, when someone does us harm, it gives us an opportunity to develop our practice of patience, which we need to bring to perfection if we are going to attain enlightenment. Therefore, ordinary enemies are really the friends of our Dharma practice. The ones who can be obstacles, however, are the people close to us, if they give us advice to seek happiness from outer sources and to act in a selfish or malicious way. Milarepa sings that he is not letting anyone close to him be an obstacle to his practice, and that is all he has. He does not have much, he sings, but at least he has that.

Sometimes the people close to us say that instead of practicing Dharma, we should be accumulating wealth. They say that we should be protecting and looking after our friends and overcoming our enemies. That kind of advice can be an obstacle to our Dharma practice if we follow it. Therefore, when we are practicing the Dharma, we should see this life to be like an illusion and a dream, and have compassion that includes both friends and enemies in equal measure. Then we will be practicing Dharma authentically.

THE GURU'S INSTRUCTIONS
AND ONE'S OWN INTELLIGENCE

Outside my father, the lama is shining
While my own knowledge cleans the stains up inside
And in between, confident understanding starts to gleam
I've got no doubts about Dharma—that's all I've got!

In the first line of this verse, Milarepa sings about meeting his teacher (Tib.: *lama*, or Skt.: *guru*), Marpa the Translator. Milarepa had studied with a few other teachers before he met Marpa. He trained in black magic with Khulung-pa Yönten Gyamtso and Yungtön Trog-yal. But after he cast his spells and devastated his village, he began to intensely regret the awful things he had done. His mind was so dis-turbed by this regret that he could not eat during the day, and he could not sleep during the night. So Yungtön Trogyal advised him to practice Dharma in order to purify his negative actions, gain libera-tion, and help all sentient beings do the same.

When Milarepa said that he would indeed like to do this, Yungtön Trogyal sent him to a Dzogchen teacher named Rongtön Lhaga. Rongtön Lhaga told Milarepa: "My Dzogchen teachings are so amaz-ing that if one meditates on them during the day, one will become a buddha during the day; if one meditates on them at night, one will become a buddha at night; and some very fortunate ones of the high-est acumen do not even have to meditate—just hearing the teachings is enough for them to gain liberation."

Milarepa thought to himself, "I was so good at casting spells that I must be one of the fortunate disciples who do not need to medi-tate," and he spent a few days just sleeping. But when he returned to see Rongtön Lhaga and had no experiences or realizations to re-port, Rongtön Lhaga said: "Perhaps I cannot help you after all, and in any event, perhaps I have praised my teachings too highly. You should go see Marpa the Translator, a siddha of the Secret Vajra-yana's new translation school.* He has been your teacher for many lifetimes."

Just from hearing Marpa's name, Milarepa was filled with inex-pressible joy, his skin broke out in goose bumps, and he cried tears of devotion. He went in search of Marpa, and when he actually saw his

* In Tibet, there were two eras of translation of the Buddhist tantras. According to the *Great Tibetan-Chinese Dictionary* (electronic edition; Tibetan title: *tshig mdzod chen mo;* Kathmandu: Padma Karpo Translation Committee, 1995) the "old translation school" began with the Indian pandit and translator Kusara in the seventh century, and the "new translation school" began with the Tibetan translator Rinchen Zangpo in the eleventh century. The old translation school's works are esteemed by the Nyingma lineage of Tibetan Buddhism, whereas the other three main lineages—Geluk, Kagyu, and Sakya—rely on the works produced by the new translation school.

guru for the first time, he was stunned, overcome by incredible joy. Then Marpa put Milarepa through many difficult ordeals, and finally, like one crystal vessel pouring all the nectar inside it into another, Marpa gave him empowerments, transmissions, and teachings in a complete and perfect way. That is what one needs as the outer condition—to meet a qualified teacher and to receive their teachings.

At the same time, one also needs the inner condition, which Milarepa sings about in the second line: "My own knowledge cleans the stains up inside." The stains refer to the obscurations of the disturbing emotions (desire, anger, stupidity, pride, and jealousy are the root disturbing emotions), and the cognitive obscurations that block omniscience. We could also describe the stains as the mistaken beliefs that the self truly exists and that phenomena truly exist.

No matter how great your guru is, the guru cannot remove your mental stains of clinging to things as being truly existent. You must clean up these stains with your own knowledge of emptiness, the true nature of reality. You can cultivate this knowledge, this wisdom, by listening to, reflecting on, and meditating on the teachings of the genuine Dharma. By listening, reflecting, and meditating again and again, your knowledge will grow, and gradually you will clear away the stains of clinging to things as being truly existent.

The result of that, Milarepa sings, is that "Confident understanding starts to gleam." This understanding he sings about is imbued with confidence in the Dharma; he is certain about the meaning of the genuine Dharma. He is not left wondering, "Are outer appearances truly existent, or are they dreamlike? Are disturbing emotions and suffering real, or is their abiding nature inexpressible luminous clarity? If I train in and practice the Dharma's teachings, will that lead me to liberation from confusion and suffering, or not?" Milarepa is sure about the answers to these questions, so he sings in the last line, "I've got no doubts about Dharma—that's all I've got!" Here, he is singing in a humble way: I am not someone with high realization, I am not anyone great; all I have got is that I do not have any doubts about the Dharma.

ALL-EMBRACING COMPASSION

> Outside the six kinds of beings are shining
> Inside compassion for everyone shines
> And in between, I remember my meditation experiences
> No self-clinging, only compassion—that's all I've got!

In this fourth verse, Milarepa sings about how he gives rise to compassion, the wish that sentient beings be free from suffering, in an unbiased way. In order to be able to do this, the essential outer condition is the six kinds of sentient beings that inhabit the six realms. All these sentient beings suffer in a variety of ways, as a result of believing that they themselves and the appearances they perceive truly exist. So these confused sentient beings provide the outer focus for Milarepa's compassion.

In this way, we see that sentient beings are essential to our Dharma path. For if there were no sentient beings, we could not practice compassion, and since enlightenment is attained when a practitioner brings wisdom and compassion to perfection, there would then be no way to attain enlightenment. Therefore, we should be grateful to sentient beings for giving us the chance to cultivate compassion, as well as to practice generosity and patience, and thereby progress on the path to enlightenment. Sentient beings are what we need on the outside.

On the inside what we need is genuine, all-embracing compassion, which means compassion for everyone. Ordinarily, one only has compassion for one's friends and perhaps other people whom one likes from a distance, whom one feels are sympathetic and worthy of compassion, like the victims of aggression. In contrast, one does not usually feel compassion for one's enemies and people one does not like, whom one feels are unsympathetic, evil, or otherwise unworthy of compassion, like the perpetrators of aggressive acts. However, that is not authentic compassion. Authentic compassion includes friends and enemies, victims and aggressors, in a completely equal way; it does not have any bias in terms of having more affection for one sentient being and less for someone else.

How can we cultivate compassion even for our enemies and aggressors? In *Entering the Bodhisattvas' Way,* Shantideva teaches an excellent method based on the following hypothetical situation: Suppose someone hits you with a rod. Whom or what should you be angry at? The logical thing to be angry at is the rod itself, because it is what actually harmed you. But obviously, the rod did not hit you intentionally; it was moved by your enemy's arm. However, it is not appropriate to be angry at your enemy's arm, because it did not move intentionally; it was motivated by the anger in your enemy's mind. So then, should you be angry at that anger? The anger, too, did not arise intentionally, nor did your enemy intentionally get angry at you. We know from our own experience how miserable it feels to be angry—when you are angry, you have trouble sleeping at night and you feel terrible all day. So no one chooses to get angry. Anger arises due to ignorance, due to the mistaken belief that self and other truly exist. Since this ignorance is only the source of suffering, then those who experience it, be they our friends or our enemies, are worthy only of our compassion, not anger.

Another method for cultivating all-embracing compassion is to gain certainty in friends and enemies' true nature, which is that friends and enemies do not truly exist. Friends and enemies are mere appearances, like dreams; "friend" and "enemy" are mere labels and conceptual imputations. In genuine reality, friends and enemies are equality. The more certainty you have in that, the less that attachment to friends and anger at enemies will disturb your mind. You will regard both friends and enemies with a sense of relaxed and spacious equanimity, and from within that state, it is easy to give rise to compassion for both friends and enemies who themselves suffer from taking friends and enemies to be truly existent.

Milarepa cultivated compassion in these ways, and when he sings, "And in between, I remember my meditation experiences," he is referring to his experiences of meditating on and cultivating compassion. Remembering compassion again and again is important to making compassion grow.

As a result, Milarepa can sing: "No self-clinging, only compassion—that's all I've got!" He has compassion that is noble because it is free from selfishness. When Milarepa is compassionate toward others, he does not wish for anything for himself. He does not wish for the individual whom he has helped to reciprocate. He does not hope for any reward, fame, or even a higher level of attainment on the path of Dharma; for example, he does not think: "As a result of being compassionate in this way, I will become a noble bodhisattva." To be altruistic without hope for personal benefit is to practice authentic compassion. Milarepa sings in a humble way that he may not have much, but this much—unselfish compassion—he does have.

It is difficult as beginners to be compassionate in a way that is perfectly all-embracing and unselfish. So if you notice that you have thoughts of bias or selfishness, do not be discouraged. Simply recall that in genuine reality, the selfish and biased individual does not truly exist, and selfish and biased thoughts do not truly exist either. Then meditate by resting your mind within that certainty in the true nature of reality. When you do this, you will be training in emptiness and compassion in union.

Compassion is the very foundation of Mahayana practice, because in order to enter the Mahayana, one must first give rise to relative bodhichitta, the wish to attain enlightenment for the benefit of all sentient beings. We give rise to this bodhichitta by engendering compassion that encompasses all sentient beings. When we do that, it feels like all sentient beings are right here, right now, and we want to do everything we can to free them from their suffering. Only when our compassion is strong like this can we engender the wish to attain enlightenment for everyone's benefit. That is why compassion is the root of Mahayana practice.

We find evidence of the power of Milarepa's noble compassion in many places in his life story. For example, once when Milarepa was meditating in the forest, a frightened stag ran across his path. Milarepa felt great compassion for the stag, so in a soothing and beautiful voice, he sang the stag a song of Dharma teaching. This assuaged the stag's fear, and he sat down right at Milarepa's feet. A short time later, there came a ferocious hunting dog in chase of the stag. Out of his great compassion Milarepa sang the hunting dog a song, which completely dissolved her anger and ferocity. She whimpered, licked Milarepa's robes, and sat down right next to the stag as if they were mother and child. Finally there came the hunter, an angry person to begin with, but who became even angrier when he saw his dog sitting next to the stag. He looked at Milarepa and he was sure that Milarepa was a black magician who had cast a spell on his dog. So he drew an arrow from his quiver and was about to shoot Milarepa, but Milarepa did not get angry or frightened, he simply said: "Man, there is plenty of time for you to shoot your arrow, so first please allow for some time to listen to my song." And Milarepa's song affected the hunter so much that he dropped his arrow, which he had never done before. He eventually became one of Milarepa's best students.

This story and others like it illustrate the power of Milarepa's all-embracing compassion. For how was it that time and again, even Milarepa's enemies who intended to do him great harm became his students? It was because of Milarepa's tremendous compassion.

SELF-LIBERATED APPEARANCES, SELF-ARISEN WISDOM

Outside the three realms are shining in freedom
Inside the wisdom, self-arisen, shines
And in between is the confidence of realizing basic being
I've got no fear of the true meaning—that's all I've got!

In this verse Milarepa sings about his realization of the true nature of reality. To realize the true nature of reality, the necessary outer condition is for the "three realms" to be "shining in freedom." The three realms refer to the universe and all of the sentient beings within it. Sentient beings inhabit the desire realm, the form realm, and the formless realm, so these three realms include all the experiences that one could possibly have, and they are shining in freedom—they are self-liberated.*

---

* Most sentient beings, including animals and humans, inhabit the desire realm, so named because desire for physical and mental pleasure and happiness is the overriding mental experience of beings in this realm. The form realm and the formless realm are populated by gods in various meditative states who are very attached to meditative experiences of clarity and the total absence of thoughts, respectively.

"Self-liberation" in one sense means that appearances of the three realms do not require an outside liberator to come and set them free, because freedom and purity are their very nature. This is because appearances of the three realms are not real. They are like appearances in dreams. They are the mere coming together of interdependent causes and conditions; they have no essence of their own, no inherent nature. This means that the appearances of the three realms are appearance-emptiness inseparable, and therefore, the three realms are free right where they are. Freedom is their basic reality. However, whether our experience of life in the three realms is one of freedom or bondage depends upon whether we realize their self-liberated true nature or not. It is like dreaming of being imprisoned: If you do not know you are dreaming, you will believe that your captivity is truly existent, and you will long to be liberated from it. But if you know you are dreaming, you will recognize that your captivity is a mere appearance, and that there is really no captivity at all—the captivity is self-liberated. Realizing that feels very good.

The term "self-liberation" is also used in the Mahamudra and Dzogchen teachings, which describe appearances as "self-arisen and self-liberated." This means that phenomena have no truly existent causes. For example, with a car that appears in a dream, you cannot say in which factory that car was made. Or with the person who appears in the mirror when you stand in front of it, you cannot say where that person was born. Since the dream car and the person in the mirror have no real causes for arising, all we can say about them is that they are self-arisen, and therefore they are also self-liberated.

When we apply this to an experience of suffering, we find that since our suffering has no real causes, it does not truly arise, like suffering in a dream. So it is self-arisen, and therefore it is self-liberated. Since the suffering is not really there in the first place, it is pure and free all by itself. And apart from knowing self-liberation is suffering's essential nature and resting within that, we do not need to do anything to alleviate it.

Thus, Milarepa sings that what one needs on the inside is to realize self-arisen original wisdom. This wisdom is the basic nature of mind, the basic nature of reality, and all outer appearances are this wisdom's own energy and play. Original wisdom is self-arisen in the sense that it is not something created; it does not come from causes and conditions; it does not arise anew, because it has been present since beginningless time as the basic nature of what we are. We just have to realize it. The realization of original wisdom, however, transcends there being anything to realize and anyone who realizes something, because original wisdom transcends duality.

How can we gain certainty about and cultivate our experience of this wisdom? Since wisdom is the true nature of mind, begin by looking at your mind. When you look at your mind, you do not see anything. You do not see any shape or color, or anything that you could identify as a "thing." When you try to locate where your mind is, you cannot find it inside your body, outside your body, nor anywhere in between. So mind is unidentifiable and unfindable. If you then rest in this unfindability, you experience mind's natural luminous clarity. That is the beginning of the experience of original wisdom. For Milarepa, original wisdom is shining. It is manifesting brightly through his realization of the nature of the three realms and of his own mind.

In the third line, Milarepa sings of his confidence of realizing the true nature of reality, the true meaning. There are the expressions and words that we use to describe things, and the meaning that these words refer to—here Milarepa is singing about the latter. He is certain about the basic nature of reality, and as he sings in the fourth line, he has no fear of it, no doubts about what it is. He is also not afraid of the truth and reality of emptiness. When he sings: "that's all I've got," he is saying: "I am not somebody great. I do not have a high realization. All I have got is this much." This is Milarepa's way of being humble.

One can easily be frightened by teachings on emptiness. It is easy to think: "Everything is empty, so I am all alone in an infinite vacuum of empty space." If you have that thought, it is a sign that you need to meditate more on the selflessness of the individual. If you think of yourself as something while everything else is nothing, it is easy to get a feeling of being alone in empty space. However, if you remember that all phenomena, including you yourself, are equally of the nature of emptiness, beyond the concepts of "something" and "nothing," then you will not be lonely; you will be open, spacious, and relaxed.

In the context of this verse, it is helpful to consider a stanza from the *Song of Mahamudra* by Jamgön Kongtrül Lodrö Thaye:

> From mind itself, so difficult to describe,
> Samsara and nirvana's magical variety shines.
> Knowing it is self-liberated is view supreme.

"Mind itself," the true nature of mind, original wisdom, is difficult to describe—it is inexpressible. And from this inexpressible true nature of mind come all the appearances of samsara and nirvana. Appearances do not exist separately from the mind. What appears has no nature of its own. Appearances are merely mind's own energy; mind's own radiance; mind's own light. And so appearances are a magical display. To describe the appearances of samsara and nirvana as a magical variety means that they are not real—they are magic, like a magician's illusions. Appearances are the magical display of the energy of the inexpressible true nature of mind. When we know this, we know that appearances are self-arisen and self-liberated, and that is the supreme view we can have.

Sense Experience and the Conduct of Equal Taste

> Outside the five sense pleasures are shining
> Inside the wisdom, free of clinging, shines
> And in between is conduct where everything tastes the same
> I am not thinking joy and pain are different things—that's all I am!

In this verse Milarepa sings of the conduct of equal taste and how to practice it. What we need on the outside to practice equal taste are the five objects of sense experience: pleasant and unpleasant forms that appear to our eyes; sounds that we think are pleasant and unpleasant; smells that we enjoy and that we find revolting; tastes that we like and do not like; and finally inner and outer bodily sensations that feel good and bad.

The conduct of equal taste sees all of these experiences to be equal, in the sense that they all equally lack inherent existence. They are all equally appearance-emptiness. Because Milarepa realizes this, he sings that on the inside he abides in wisdom—wisdom that realizes emptiness. This wisdom is therefore free of clinging—free from attachment to sense experiences as being real. When we think that good experiences are real, we get attached to them and want more; when we think bad experiences are real, we are averse to them and want them to disappear. That way of adopting what we fancy and rejecting what we do not is completely opposite to the conduct of equal taste. On the other hand, when we realize that none of these experiences are truly existent, the conduct of equal taste naturally follows from that realization.

The conduct of equal taste is very similar to the conduct one performs in a dream when one knows one is dreaming. When we dream and do not recognize it, although the sensory objects that appear are not truly existent, we do not know that and we cling to them as being real. However, when we recognize that we are dreaming, we abide in the wisdom that realizes sense objects are dependently arisen mere appearances, appearance-emptiness inseparable, and we are free of clinging and attachment. When that happens, whatever sensory objects appear, they do not cause us suffering.

As a result of realizing sense experiences are appearance-emptiness and performing the conduct of equal taste, Milarepa does not think joy and pain are different things. He is neither attached to being happy nor afraid of being in pain. He knows that in genuine reality, joy and pain are equality. Milarepa does not differentiate between joy and pain like ordinary people do, because he realizes their basic nature. Milarepa demonstrated this many times, and it is good to look at Milarepa's life story to see how he practiced equal taste and realized the equality of joy and pain. At the end of the verse, Milarepa sings, as a way of preventing himself from being arrogant, that realization of joy and pain's equality is "all I've got!"

Freedom from Hope and Fear

Outside creations are shining in ruins
Inside the freedom from hope and fear shines
And in between, I'm not sick with striving or straining, no, no, no!
I am not thinking right and wrong are two different things—
    that's all I am!

How is Milarepa able to achieve freedom from the fixations that produce hope and fear? First, he sees that on the outside, "creations are shining in ruins." This means that Milarepa knows that whatever appears on the outside is impermanent, because all things are creations or composites of causes and conditions. When a particular thing's causes and conditions change, that thing will fall apart. Sentient beings make problems for themselves when they think that appearances will last; that the situations they find themselves in are permanent and unchanging. In fact, whatever we do or create, whatever situation we are in, and even we ourselves have no power to remain. Everything is subject to decay.

Realizing that, on the inside Milarepa is free from hope and fear. He is not attached to outer appearances as being permanent, so he has no hope that things will remain nor fear that they will not; no hope that things will come out one way nor fear that they will not.

Then in between, Milarepa sings of how it is a sickness when, while meditating on the genuine nature of reality, one tries to make something happen or tries to change or improve things. The true nature of reality transcends all concepts of what it might be; it is inexpressible and inconceivable. Therefore, the true nature transcends improvement and degradation. So the way to meditate on it is to simply relax within it, free from striving and straining. That is how Milarepa is—he is able to rest in the basic nature of reality in a spacious, uncontrived, natural way.

These first three lines reveal how Milarepa practiced Dharma at the end of his life. When it was time for Milarepa to pass away, he did not suffer, because he knew that his body and life were subject to decay. Therefore, he had no hope to live forever and no fear of dying. He did not strive or strain to avoid death. He meditated on death's true nature, which transcends even the concept of death, and so he experienced his death as simply another manifestation of the true nature of mind's energy and play. Unlike ordinary beings, for Milarepa death was not frightening; it was blissful.

At the end of the verse, Milarepa sings, "I am not thinking right and wrong are two different things—that's all I am!" Milarepa does not deny that there is any difference between right and wrong, between positive actions and negative ones. Rather, he is free of thinking that right and wrong truly exist. He is free of attachment to right and wrong as having any inherent nature—he knows they are dependently arisen mere appearances.

The way that ordinary people relate to right and wrong, good and bad, and virtue and nonvirtue is to believe that they are real. This is just how someone would relate to a dream of good and bad actions when they did not know that they were dreaming. However, when one realizes the nature of emptiness, one relates to virtue and non-virtue in a different way, understanding them to be mere appearances that do not truly exist, just as one would during a dream when one knew that one was dreaming. That is Milarepa's perspective.

That is why karma, right, wrong, virtue, and nonvirtue only exist for ordinary sentient beings who have not directly realized the true nature of reality. In contrast, the noble ones, who directly realize the true nature, transcend all concepts of right and wrong. As the Buddha taught in the sutras: "For those belonging to the family of the noble ones, karmic actions do not exist, and results of karmic actions do not exist, either."* Since the noble ones have purified themselves of clinging to true existence, they transcend the concepts of virtue and nonvirtue.

The Indian master Aryadeva explained that there are three levels of teachings about virtue and nonvirtue:

* Khenpo Tsültrim Gyamtso, *The Sun of Wisdom* (Boston: Shambhala Publications, 2003), p. 109.

First, the lack of virtue is counteracted,
Second, the self is counteracted and,
Finally, all views are counteracted.

The first level's purpose is to reverse the tendency beginning students have to do things that are negative. In order to accomplish this, students are taught the benefits of performing good actions that are helpful to others, and the suffering that comes from doing bad things that are harmful to others.

At this stage, virtue and nonvirtue's true nature—emptiness—is not taught. Furthermore, in order to have a basis for the explanation that there is an actor who performs actions and experiences their results, the self is described as if it exists. The self is the one who performs actions, good or bad, and then experiences happiness or suffering respectively as a result.

Once students have gained confidence that it is important to perform positive actions and refrain from negative ones, they are introduced to the second level, whose purpose is to reverse the students' clinging to a truly existent self. Students are taught how to analyze the self and determine that the self does not exist in genuine reality. From this, they understand that there cannot be any truly existent virtuous or nonvirtuous actions either, because there is no truly existent actor to perform them. At this stage, virtue and nonvirtue are taught to be nonexistent in genuine reality.

Then, when students have gained certainty in selflessness and emptiness, they are introduced to the third level, whose function is to reverse clinging to any view or reference point at all, even the views of emptiness and selflessness. This level leads students to the realization that reality transcends all of our concepts about what it might be, whether they be concepts of existence, nonexistence, emptiness, or anything else. At this point, we are taught that even the more subtle understanding that we had at the second stage, of things not truly existing, cannot accurately describe the true nature of reality, which lies beyond all concepts. So we transcend even the idea of nonexistence, even the idea of emptiness.

QUESTIONS AND ANSWERS

Question: Why in the song is everything "shining"?

Khenpo Tsültrim Gyamtso Rinpoche: Everything is shining because the true nature of mind is luminous clarity, the buddha nature, Mahamudra, and all appearances are that luminous clarity's own energy, radiance, and light. When sunlight is refracted through a colored crystal, and rainbows shine on the walls of the room, that is an example of the relationship between mind and appearances. And furthermore, the true nature of mind is naturally shining and naturally liberated.

At the Dharma center where I am staying,* in the shrine room there are beautiful crystal offering lamps of many different colors. Each offering lamp's light mixes and plays with the light of the others to create even more changing, beautiful colors. I think those are the best offering lamps I have ever seen. If you look at those beautiful lights, you get a good example of how appearances are naturally shining and naturally liberated, self-arisen and self-liberated. You cannot find any real reason for why the lights appear—they do not have any truly existent causes and conditions. So the appearances themselves do not really exist. What are they then? Self-arisen; and since they are self-arisen, they are self-liberated. These qualities of appearances are important to know: they are luminous and shining, self-arisen and self-liberated.

Our teacher, the Buddha, looked with his eye of wisdom and did not see a single truly existent cause or condition. Therefore, he taught that all phenomena are appearance-emptiness, like in a dream. The ultimate way to express this is to say that phenomena are self-arisen and self-liberated.

Q: I have a question about two incidents from Milarepa's life story. Once he was mending his robes when he thought to himself: "Everything is impermanent, and I may die tonight. So there is no point in mending these robes." Another time, Milarepa sang: "Going, wandering, sleeping,

---

* Karma Thegsum Chöling, Shamong, New Jersey.

resting, I look at mind. This is virtuous practice without sessions or breaks."

These two events seem contradictory. If you can practice Dharma by looking at your mind during all activities, so that you are always performing virtue, what is wrong with mending clothes? On the other hand, if mending clothes is really useless, then are all ordinary activities useless?

KTGR: These were different situations where Milarepa was emphasizing specific aspects of the teachings in each one. In the first situation, Milarepa was training in impermanence in order to reverse his clinging to things as permanent.

In the second situation, Milarepa was teaching that the true nature of mind is Mahamudra, and the way to practice Mahamudra meditation is to look at the true nature of mind again and again during all daily activities. Whether you are going, wandering, sleeping, or resting, look directly at the nature of mind, and let go and relax. That is the practice of Mahamudra that transcends the duality and limitation of meditation "sessions" and "breaks" from those sessions. It is continuous meditation.

So there was no contradiction between these two teachings—they are both very good.

Q: It was mentioned that Milarepa remained in a state of equal taste, and I was just wondering how you ever get there, because sensations are so overwhelming. For example, when you eat something you do not like, you can conceptually tell yourself: "Oh, it is not so bad and I should really think of the true nature of things." But yet you sort of cringe—you have a strong physical response. So can Rinpoche please give some suggestions of what to actually do with unpleasant sense experiences?

KTGR: We must proceed step-by-step. First, we need the view of emptiness. All phenomena are empty of essence—they are empty of there being any actual identity to them.

We also need the view of equality. In *The Noble Sutra of the Ten Grounds,* the Buddha taught ten types of equality—ten ways that all phenomena are equal.* Three of these are most important: First, in terms of genuine reality, all things are equal in that the true nature of each one of them equally transcends any concept about what it might be. Second, also with reference to their genuine nature, all phenomena are equal because they are all originally and perfectly pure—since beginningless time the nature of all phenomena is perfect purity. Finally, in terms of apparent reality, the appearances of all phenomena are equal because all appearances are equally like dreams, illusions, and water-moons. Certainty in this view of emptiness and equality is the first thing you need in order to start developing the conduct of equal taste.

Even though the term that is used is equal taste, it is not the usual use of the word "taste"—rather, it is a quality that applies not only to the sense experiences but to all experiences. It means to know that friends and enemies are of the nature of equality and that happiness and suffering are of the nature of equality. We can understand this more easily if we think of the example of a dream. If you dream and you do not know that you are dreaming, and you eat something that tastes good and then something else that tastes bad, then because you do not know you are dreaming, you think that these experiences are real and very different. Once you know that you are dreaming, however, you know that both the appearance of a good taste and of a bad one are not real; that they are just mere appearances. So you know there is actually no difference between them at all—they are equality. As for the ultimate reality of the dream, it transcends the concepts of existence and nonexistence both. The actual reality of the dream is beyond all concept of what it might be.

So initially, we need to gain certainty in this view. We need to analyze in order to understand it and to be free of doubt that this is in

* The quotation from this sutra enumerating the ten types of equality, along with explanatory notes, can be found in *The Moon of Wisdom: Chapter Six of Chandrakirti's* Entering the Middle Way (Ithaca, N.Y.: Snow Lion Publications, 2005), p. 29.

fact how things are. Then in meditation we rest in that certainty, we cultivate that certainty again and again. Then we can begin to experience equal taste. That is how the process works.

For beginners, which means all ordinary sentient beings, we who are not noble bodhisattvas, there is no direct realization of equal taste. Beginners can, however, make preparations that lead to direct realization by listening to teachings about equal taste and reflecting on it. Through these two activities of listening and reflecting, we develop our knowledge of the true nature of reality, and we can give rise to certainty that this is really the way it is. Then when we meditate we can start to gain some experience of it. When this experience becomes direct realization, one becomes a noble bodhisattva.

Think about the stages of the dream: when you do not know that you are dreaming; when you know that you are dreaming; and the ultimate nature of the dream. Thinking of the dream example will also help you to gain certainty.

Q: If what you said about virtue and nonvirtue is true, then one might assume that nothing really matters.

KTGR: That way of thinking denies even the appearance of virtue and nonvirtue. It holds that not only do virtue and nonvirtue not exist genuinely or ultimately, but they do not even appear. The authentic view does not do that; rather, the authentic view explains that virtue and nonvirtue are dependently arisen mere appearances that have no inherent nature. It is not that there are no appearances of virtue and nonvirtue, because they do appear. Thus, virtue and nonvirtue appear but they do not truly exist, so they are dependently arisen mere appearances, just like the virtue and nonvirtue that appear in dreams.

The genuine nature of reality transcends karma, cause and result, and good and bad. In apparent reality, however, there are appearances of good and bad, of positive actions leading to happiness, and of negative actions producing suffering. It is beyond doubt that in apparent reality, positive actions produce happiness and negative actions produce suffering.

To say that something is a dependently arisen mere appearance is a very important part of the view, so we should understand what that means. The example we can use to help us understand dependent arising is the water-moon. If you have a clear lake, a clear sky that is free of clouds, and the moon in the sky, then on the surface of that lake you will have an appearance of the moon. The water-moon does not inherently exist; it is a mere appearance that manifests due to the coming together of causes and conditions. In the same way, the appearances of this lifetime, the causes that we accumulate for the appearances of our future lifetimes, and everything that happened in past lifetimes, are all dependently arisen mere appearances, manifesting due to the coming together of different causes and conditions, lacking self-nature, like water-moons.

Q: What strikes me so much about what you told us is actually the story about the stag, dog, and hunter. What I am really impressed by is the skill in teaching to each of those, even more so than I am impressed by the wonderful level of realization of Milarepa. So my question is: How can we cultivate those skillful means in ourselves given that we are struggling with our own level of realization? How can we cultivate that ability to help others ripen and to realize the nature of their own true existence?

KTGR: One of the best things you can do to help others realize their own nature, whether they are beginners or old students or anywhere in between, is the practices known as *lojong,* or *The Seven Points of Mind Training.* The *Mind Training* teachings begin with a brief but profound explanation of ultimate bodhichitta—emptiness. Then they go into extensive detail about how to give rise to relative bodhichitta, loving-kindness, and compassion. In order to develop the ability to help others to realize their own nature, we need both the ultimate and relative aspects of bodhichitta.

That is why the Mahayana is the practice of emptiness and compassion together. As a beginner, one cannot give rise to the direct realization of emptiness right away, which is why in the *Mind Training*
teachings, emptiness is only taught in a concise way at the outset.
However, what one can definitely do as a beginner is give rise to compassion. That is why *Mind Training* teaches compassion in a much
more extensive way. By combining the two together, the brief explanation of how to meditate on emptiness and the extensive explanation of how to give rise to loving-kindness and compassion, one can
learn how to practice on the Mahayana path of emptiness and compassion together.

The *Mind Training* teachings on compassion describe the practice
of sending and taking (Tib.: *tonglen*), and whether one is experiencing
happiness or suffering, one should do this practice. "Sending and taking should be practiced alternately. The two should ride the breath," is
what the teaching says. When you exhale, you send out all of your happiness and virtue to others in the form of bright light, and when you
inhale, you take into yourself all of their suffering and negativity in the
form of dark smoke and purify them in your heart, which you imagine
to be a bright sphere of pure light, inseparable from emptiness.

The teachings also say: "When you are happy, knowing that happiness is appearance-emptiness, give your happiness to all sentient
beings. When you are suffering, knowing that your suffering is appearance-emptiness, take all sentient beings' suffering on yourself."
This is called the practice that keeps you from getting too high or too
low—in other words, you will not get too distracted by happiness, or
too discouraged by suffering.

The *Mind Training* teachings have been translated and explained
in many books. You should read them again and again, particularly
the root verses. The more you read them, the more your certainty in
them will grow.

Q: When your teacher gives you the instructions pointing out the
nature of your mind, how is it possible to ascertain the difference
between "getting it" and just fantasizing about getting it?

KTGR: If the true nature of reality could really be pointed out, it would be some truly existent and identifiable entity; but it is beyond that. The true nature of reality transcends being an object of recognition, so it cannot actually be pointed out. Therefore, the true nature is beyond "getting it" or not.

Pointing out instructions are only given in traditions that assert self-awareness. Therefore, when these instructions are given, what is pointed out is just your own mind experiencing itself. So you can look at your own experience of your mind to see whether you recognize its true nature or not; but remember that there is nothing really there to get, and no one really there to get it or not. The true nature of mind is beyond that.

The Eighth Karmapa,* Mikyö Dorje, taught that if you have very clear certainty that your mind does not truly arise, abide, or cease, that is what it means to "recognize" your mind's true nature; that is what it means to "get" the pointing out instruction. His definition of recognizing mind's true nature is in harmony with the middle turning of the wheel of Dharma's teachings.

From the perspective of the traditions that assert self-awareness and self-arisen original wisdom, what is pointed out is self-experience that is nondual (meaning that there is no perceived object and no perceiving subject), nonconceptual, and unconfused.

How is this done? The teacher might ask the student: "Do you have happiness? Do you have suffering?" If the answer is "yes," then the next question is: "What is that joy like? What is that pain like? Others cannot experience your joy and pain, so you describe it." Very quickly, the student recognizes that their mind's experience of happiness and suffering are actually inexpressible. Then the teacher says: "Rest in that inexpressible self-experience." That is how nonconceptual and unconfused self-awareness is pointed out; how to recognize it; and how to rest within it.

---

* The Karmapas are the head gurus of the Karma Kagyu lineage. The current Karmapa, Ogyen Trinley Dorje, is the seventeenth in this line.

5

The Eighteen Kinds of Yogic Joy

Milarepa's Song of Realization, with Commentary

TRANSLATED BY ARI GOLDFIELD

IN A PLACE called Yolmo Gangra, high up in the Nepalese Himalayas, Milarepa sang a song of realization called *The Eighteen Kinds of Yogic Joy.* Yolmo is a sacred place, blessed by the Buddha Shakyamuni's own prophecy in *The Avatamsaka Sutra* that it would be a great land of Dharma practice. The master Padmasambhava also blessed Yolmo with his prophecy that it would be a secret place for yogis and yoginis to stay in secluded retreat. And it is an even more extraordinary place for we who follow Milarepa's lineage, because Marpa the King of Translators prophesied that Milarepa would go there to practice.

THE EIGHTEEN KINDS OF YOGIC JOY

I bow at the feet of the genuine guru
Because of merit gathered, I've met this lord
The guru with his prophecy is what has brought me here
My comfortable castle, this wooded mountain range
This is a meadowland so beautiful in bloom
The trees are dancing in the midst of all the trees

This is a place of play, where the monkeys and the langurs play
A place where birds speak in bird-like tongues
A land of flying bees on gentle wings
Where day runs into night, and rainbow paintings shine
Summer runs into winter, a light drizzle falls
Autumn runs into springtime, the mist comes rolling in

In a solitary place like this, I the yogi Milarepa
Am feeling very clear light well, meditating on emptiness mind
When I get a lot of stuff coming up, I feel extremely well
When the highs roll into lows, feels even better still
Feels so good to be a human being without the karmic deeds
When confusion gets complicated, I feel extremely well

Fearsome visions getting worse and worse feels even better still
Kleshas, birth and death, and freedom from those is a good way to feel
With the bullies getting worse and worse, I feel extremely well
When there's not a painful illness in sight, feels even better still
The suffering being bliss feels so good that feeling bad feels good
Since the trulkhor comes from what I am, it feels extremely good

To leap and run about is dance—feels even better still
To be a king of speech with a treasury of song feels good
That the words are like the buzzing of bees feels extremely good
That the sound it makes is merit collecting feels even better still
The bliss is good in the expanse of the confidence of strength of mind
What develops on its own by its own force feels extremely good

What comes out looking like a hodgepodge feels even better still
This happy experience song by a yogi carefree
Is for you who believe in what you're doing here
To take along with you when you go*

* This song was translated under the guidance of Khenpo Tsültrim Gyamtso Rinpoche by Jim Scott in 1994. The original Tibetan source is *Mi la ras pa'i rnam mgur* (n.p.: mtsho sngon mi rigs dpe skrun khang, 1989), pp. 255–56.

The Joy of the Student-Teacher Relationship

> I bow at the feet of the genuine guru
> Because of merit gathered, I've met this lord
> The guru with his prophecy is what has brought me here

Milarepa begins by paying homage to Marpa, his glorious and genuine guru, by bowing at Marpa's feet with his body, speech, and mind filled with great respect. Milarepa then describes how he has fulfilled Marpa's prophecy that he would come to practice in Yolmo, which makes him very happy. At the same time, Milarepa knows that he was able to receive and fulfill Marpa's prophecy because he had accumulated the merit necessary to meet his teacher.

When we meet an authentic spiritual teacher, if we develop certainty, trust, and faith in this guru, that is a sign that in past lifetimes we have performed many positive and altruistic actions and thereby have accumulated great merit. Otherwise, perhaps we might place our faith in an inauthentic teacher or else meet an authentic teacher but not have faith in him or her. And if one does not have confidence in a teacher, one will not follow their guidance. Thus, meeting an authentic teacher and also having enough confidence and faith in them to follow their teachings is a sign of our karmic good fortune.

It is important to remember that when good things happen to us it is not because of blind luck or because we are "special" and deserving; rather, it is because we have performed positive actions in the past. Remembering that will prevent us from becoming arrogant or complacent as a result of our good situation, and will inspire us to continue to act in an altruistic way.

And so, these first lines of the song about Milarepa meeting his teacher, having accumulated the merit to do so, and now realizing his teacher's prophecy by coming here to practice, are Milarepa's expression of joy in his knowledge of how fortunate he is.

The Joy of the Place of Dharma Practice

My comfortable castle, this wooded mountain range

The forests in the Himalayan regions, including Yolmo, are sometimes described as looking like castles because all the trees grow thick and close together. There are vast forests and great snow mountains there, and Milarepa sings of it as "my comfortable castle" because he has arrived at this place that he considers his home. Also, he did not have to do anything to construct this home, and he does not have to do anything to try to keep it—there is no upkeep involved while he stays there. He does not have to lock the door or fix the roof; he can just live there and enjoy it. When he leaves, he can leave it just like that. That is why it is such a comfortable home for him.

What is amazing about the caves where Milarepa lived and practiced for so many years is that he did not have to build a single one of them. Even to this day, all of these caves remain intact—they are not like the ordinary homes people build, which are prone to decay. After Milarepa himself practiced in those caves, pilgrims began to visit them. They are all great places of pilgrimage for people to go and practice, even today. This is a sign of how wonderful Milarepa's homes are.

This is a meadowland, so beautiful in bloom

Those of you who have been in this Himalayan region may know that in between the forests there are vast, open plains filled with wildflowers. In particular, near Tiger Cave Lion Fortress, Milarepa's cave in Yolmo, there is a meadow called the Open Field of Great Bliss, filled with yellow, red, blue, and violet flowers—so many different kinds of flowers bloom there. It is beautiful to see.

These meadows are always changing. At one point in the year they are filled with white flowers, at another time they are filled with yellow flowers, then red flowers. They never stay the same.

The trees are dancing in the midst of all the trees

There are tall trees in the Himalayan forests, and in the summertime, when the wind blows their branches and leaves, it looks like they are swaying in dance. There are many trees bunched together, and so it looks like they are dancing together in the middle of a big party.

When you see the flowers changing color with the seasons, and the trees moving in dance like that, it is a demonstration orchestrated by the master teacher called impermanence. Flowers changing and trees swaying teach us that all things are impermanent and have no inherent nature.

> This is a place of play, where the monkeys and the langurs play
> A place where birds speak in bird-like tongues
> A land of flying bees on gentle wings

Yolmo is secluded but it is not a desolate place. It is populated by many different kinds of animals: monkeys and langurs who play around with each other in an open and carefree way; a variety of birds, each singing their own kind of beautiful song; and bees who hover and float about in a gentle way. And all of these animals are objects of our loving-kindness and compassion.

When you see monkeys, birds, and bees all just doing their own thing in an easy and free way, this is evidence of how important it is for all beings to be able to be free; to be able to live their lives not under someone else's control.

Also, when you see the suffering of these animals—the changes that their lives undergo and the suffering they experience as a result—that is a natural teaching about the suffering of samsara.

> Where day runs into night and rainbow paintings shine
> Summer runs into winter, a light drizzle falls
> Autumn runs into springtime, the mist comes rolling in
> In a solitary place like this, . . .

These lines tell us about the outer environment in Yolmo, but they also have a deeper meaning. In terms of how they describe the outer environment, "day runs into night" refers to the phenomenon in Yolmo of how the mountain peaks, covered with white snow, glow with an aura of light even at nighttime. "Summer runs into winter" and "autumn runs into springtime" describe how it is that in Yolmo there is not much difference between the seasons, between summer and winter, autumn and spring.

These lines' deeper meaning is about equality, because in genuine reality there is really no difference between day and night; and no difference between the seasons of the year. Time is of the nature of equality.

"Rainbow paintings shine" describes the beautiful rainbows that appear in the clear mountain skies, and also how it is that even though things in this life appear to be real, in fact they are not. They have no inherent nature—they are appearance-emptiness, like rainbows.

"A light drizzle falls," besides its outer meaning, is a metaphor for the clouds of the gurus' compassion pouring down the rain of blessings and teachings onto the harvest of their disciples' faith and good qualities.

When "mist comes rolling in," it covers the ground so that we cannot see things clearly. This is an example for the temporary obscurations of disturbing emotions and ignorance that prevent us from seeing the true nature of mind. And yet, because these obscurations are like mist, they have no solid essence. It is easy to clear them away.

In modern times, people like going on vacation. When they do, they enjoy going to a peaceful and beautiful place. They are conscious of what the environment is like. Milarepa is the same way—he sings about the natural environment around his cave. And the peaceful and natural environment of Yolmo is conducive to the practice of Dharma.

The wonderful thing about the natural environment is that no one owns it. One person can go and enjoy it, then someone else can go to the same place and enjoy it, and then someone else after that— everyone shares it.

Milarepa would meditate, and in between his sessions he would go out of his cave to look at the place and see what it was like. He would seek out the place's good qualities and enjoy them. At the same time, he made connections between what he saw in the dependently arisen natural environment and the profound teachings of the Dharma. So he delighted in Yolmo's beautiful qualities, but he did not cling to them as being truly existent; instead he saw them to be like dreams, illusions, rainbows, and water-moons—appearance-emptiness inseparable. In this way, Milarepa experienced the appearances that he saw as being the guru of symbolic appearances. Appearances were his teacher.

The way that Milarepa related to his surroundings teaches us well. Wherever you are, if like Milarepa you look for that place's good qualities, you will find them. You will even find that those good qualities have good qualities—more and more good qualities will manifest. This will make you happy, and the depth and stability of your meditation will grow.

Especially, you should examine your surroundings and see that from their coarse characteristics down to their most subtle aspects, they are mere appearances manifesting in dependence upon causes and conditions. When you remember this, you will remember that outer appearances are like dreams and illusions, and you will not cling to appearances as being truly existent. You will know that appearances are appearance-emptiness inseparable. You will understand the two truths: the mode of appearances that constitute relative reality; and the true nature of these appearances, emptiness, genuine reality. And since you know that appearances are appearance-emptiness inseparable, you will understand that the two truths as well are ultimately undifferentiable.

A good way to remember this is to recall these two lines that Milarepa sang on a different occasion:

E ma, the phenomena of the three realms of samsara,*
While not existing, they appear—how incredibly amazing!

---

* *E ma* is a Tibetan expression of wonderment.

At the same time we perceive appearances, what appears to us does not truly exist. Appearances' true nature is emptiness even while they appear. So appearances are appearance-emptiness inseparable, and that is incredibly amazing!

Recalling these two lines helps us to remember that appearances are not truly existent. When we remember this, rather than reinforcing our habitual pattern of thinking that things truly exist, we are putting an end to it.

This concludes the first part of the song, in which Milarepa describes the qualities of Tiger Cave Lion Fortress in Yolmo Gangra, the beautiful, peaceful, and wonderful place he is practicing. That he does not cling to Yolmo as truly existent is what makes it really wonderful. And how does he practice meditation there?

THE JOY OF MEDITATING ON THE TRUE NATURE OF MIND

Milarepa describes his meditation practice and the joy inherent within it in a simple, clear, and profound way:

> I the yogi Milarepa
> Am feeling very clear light well, meditating on emptiness mind

When meditating on the true nature of mind, the first step is to analyze mind and ascertain that mind's essence is emptiness. Once you have gained certainty in emptiness, the meditation is to simply let go and relax, free from trying to negate or affirm anything, free from trying to change or improve anything. When you do this, you can experience the natural luminous clarity that is present within mind's basic state, and that feels very good.

When you analyze your mind, you cannot find it. You cannot find it to have any shape or color. If you look for where it is right now, you cannot find it to be anywhere—you cannot find it in your brain, in your heart, or anywhere else inside or outside your body. Also, when you look directly at your mind, you cannot see it coming from or going to anywhere; and you cannot see it arising or ceasing. This is mind's emptiness—mind cannot be identified as anything; it does not have any location; it is empty of coming and going; and it is empty of arising and ceasing.

When you analyze mind and cannot find anything, this emptiness of essence actually transcends all conceptual fabrications of existence and nonexistence both. You cannot find mind to be existent anywhere, but you cannot find mind's nonexistence either. If you think you find nonexistence, then ask: "What does nonexistence look like? What are the qualities of nonexistence? Where are they to be found? Do they come or go, arise or cease?" In this way, you see that mind's true nature is beyond both the concepts of existence and nonexistence; it transcends all concepts of what it might be.

When you rest relaxed after finishing this analysis, mind is brilliant, vivid, and clear. That is mind's natural luminous clarity. This is profound: When you analyze mind, you cannot find anything; but when you rest relaxed, there is natural clarity, vividness, and bliss. There is comfort and ease—it is wonderful.

Mind's essence of inconceivable emptiness is the view emphasized by *The Transcendent Wisdom Sutras* that constitute the second turning of the wheel of Dharma. Mind's natural luminosity is taught in the third turning and the main commentaries on it, such as *The Treatise on Buddha Nature*. And when in this way we ourselves investigate mind's nature and meditate within it, we find that mind's essential emptiness and natural luminosity are inseparable. We see that the teachings of the second and third turnings are in perfect harmony. The more you meditate on mind's true nature, the more your certainty in this will grow.

When you rest in meditation like that, you experience great bliss. As Milarepa sings, "I . . . am feeling very clear light well." He experiences this natural bliss as a result of skillfully placing his mind within its natural state. This explanation comes from the Vajrayana and Mahamudra teachings about great bliss. When you put it all together it is amazing, because this one line, "Am feeling very clear light well, meditating on emptiness mind" contains the view of the second turning of the wheel of Dharma, the third turning, Vajrayana, and Mahamudra all in one.

Thoughts, Emotions, and Experiences' Variety Enhances Meditation

When I get a lot of stuff coming up, I feel extremely well

What happens when many different feelings, thoughts, and experiences seem to manifest all at once? Are these not obstacles to meditation? No, and in fact they make meditation even better! This is why Milarepa sings, "When I get a lot of stuff coming up, I feel extremely well." Not only does he feel well when he has a lot of stuff coming up, he feels *extremely* well. He feels so good because all the stuff coming up for him shines as a friend of his meditation.

For example, with feelings: When you meditate, at different times you can feel good, bad, or indifferent. However, the basic nature of all these feelings is equality. Whenever feelings arise, therefore, they shine as equality's radiance. They are an opportunity for us to realize the equality that is their essential nature, and so they are equality's friends.

With thoughts, sometimes we think noble thoughts of compassion, loving-kindness, faith, and diligence; at other times we have ignoble thoughts of attachment, anger, jealousy, and pride. All of these thoughts, both the good and the bad, are equally of the nature of clear light, luminous clarity. Therefore, whatever thought arises, it is a friend of realizing mind's nature, luminous clarity.

We also perceive a variety of outer appearances. These are like appearances in a dream. They are not a hindrance at all. In fact, they help us recognize that appearances' nature is appearance-emptiness. For example, if you dream and you want to recognize that you are dreaming, you need some appearances to recognize as being a dream. And once you have recognized you are dreaming, if you want to play and have a good time, you need something to play with! So you need all different kinds of forms, sounds, smells, tastes, and bodily sensations. Thus, all the different kinds of empty appearances are, in fact, very good because they only aid the realization that a dream is just a dream, and that the daytime is just like a dream.

Therefore, whatever kinds of empty forms might appear, whatever kinds of empty sounds you might hear, there is no need to try to stop them, nor any need to try to cause them to manifest. Whatever happens, it is all just a good focus for your meditative concentration. It provides your meditation with a supporting focus, which is good. So whatever appears, bring it into your meditation.

When the highs roll into lows, feels even better still

Sometimes the stuff we get coming up is good stuff and sometimes it is lousy. Sometimes we feel great and sometimes we feel terrible. What does Milarepa have to say about these fluctuations in how we feel, these highs rolling into lows? Not only are they good, they are even *better*. It is even *better* when feelings change from good to bad and vice versa.

For example, when you dream and you know you are dreaming, you can soar high up into the sky—a fantastic feeling. Then you can turn around and do a nosedive smack into an ocean of water, or a hot pit of fire, but it does not matter! It is just another wonderful feeling that you get to experience. You get to have all kinds of experiences, and they are all wonderful.

When you dream, you can go to a beautiful garden party where there are exquisite tables of food, musicians playing beautiful music, and people dressed elegantly, singing, dancing, and having a good time. Then you can go to a cesspool filled with excrement that smells disgusting. When you do not know you are dreaming, these two sets of appearances seem completely different. But when you know you are dreaming, the party and the cesspool are equally wonderful. You can just dive in the cesspool—how fantastic it is! It is all just a dream, and you know it.

When you realize that all appearances are like a dream, it is important to have a wide range of experiences, both ones that feel good and ones that feel bad, so that you can recognize their basic nature is equality and luminous clarity.

Feels so good to be a human being without the karmic deeds

Milarepa feels good to be living a life of genuine meaning. He is not doing anything harmful to others, so he is not accumulating negative karma. Not only that, he is cultivating wisdom and compassion so that he can be of benefit to others. When you do things with an altruistic motivation, you feel happy.

THE JOY OF MEDITATING ON CONFUSION'S TRUE NATURE

When confusion gets complicated, I feel extremely well

Many types of confusion and agitation can arise in the mind due to a variety of causes, such as: the body; material enjoyments, either having them or not; anger that arises toward enemies; attachment to friends; and work—perhaps one does not have work, or one has work and then loses it, or one works but worries that one is not working well. So many different things disturb the mind, and they are all completely wonderful, because the basic nature of the disturbed mind is peace.

This can be presented concisely using a logical reasoning: The various types of mental agitation feel wonderful when you realize their true nature, because their basic nature is equality, and equality is naturally wonderful.

In a dream, the way you get agitated because of someone you do not like is different from the way you get agitated as a result of someone you like. But both of these types of agitation are of the nature of equality, because it is just a dream.

One of the ways that all phenomena are equal is that the basic nature of every phenomenon is equally beyond any concept of what it might be. Therefore, in their true nature, confusion and agitation are equally inconceivable. When we gain certainty in that, and then rest within that certainty, our experience is open, spacious, and relaxed.

This is why our confusion is marvelous and our mental agitation is marvelous. Their kindness toward us is incredible. They are like the guru who helps us find the correct view; like friends of meditation who help us to meditate on equality.

FEAR IS GOOD

Fearsome visions getting worse and worse feels even better still

What is it like to be really scared, to experience powerful fear and anxiety? It is even better! It is even better than mental confusion. The reason for this is that the fear we experience is like being frightened in a dream. However many thoughts we have of being frightened in a dream, the basic nature of those thoughts of fear transcends fear.

Fear is good because we do not like it, and so when fear arises our discomfort with it causes us to look hard for its true nature. The way to do this is to ask: "Who is the one who is afraid? Where is the self that experiences fear?" Looking for the self in this way and not finding anything, we discover the selflessness of the individual. Then, if we analyze the thing or person we are afraid of, we discover its emptiness, and that is the emptiness of phenomena.

Finally, we look for the frightened mind and cannot find it. The frightened mind does not have any shape or color. It cannot be found anywhere inside our body or outside of it. It does not come from anywhere—fear in the mind does not exist in some other place, then come to our mind, and then go somewhere else. Since fear does not come from anywhere to our mind, and does not go anywhere from our mind, how could it really be in our mind now at all? And when we look directly at the fear in our mind, we cannot see it arising or ceasing. So we discover that the frightened mind's basic nature is Mahamudra, beyond identity, location, coming and going, and arising and ceasing. The frightened mind's essence transcends fear, so it is naturally open, spacious, and relaxed. Nothing needs to be added to it, and nothing needs to be removed from it—it is naturally blissful.

Therefore, fear is wonderful. As a result of being afraid, we can realize the individual's selflessness; phenomena's emptiness; and Mahamudra, the true nature of mind. We can realize fear's true nature, great bliss. So not only is fear great, it is *greater* than great!

You may have heard of the practice of Chö (cutting through). The point of this practice is to give rise to fear and realize its true nature. So when you practice Chö, the first thing you do is go somewhere where you are going to be frightened. In Tibet, practitioners would go alone to charnel grounds at night and sleep there. These charnel grounds are quite fearsome places. They are in isolated locations and are filled with decomposing corpses still in their clothes, skulls that still have hair, and bones all over the place. They are visited by wild carnivorous animals, spirits, and demons.

The point of the practice is to go to a place like that and get scared; and then look at the one who is afraid, at what is producing the fear, and at the frightened mind itself. If that is your practice, then you want to be afraid. It is good to be afraid. So when you get frightened, you feel great!

From analyzing fear and seeing the result of that analysis, when we ask the question "Is there any good reason to be scared?" we can find no valid reason for our fear. Then we can relax. As we have seen, there are valid reasons for fearlessness, and these are what we need to realize.

A Warrior Free from Birth, Aging, and Death

Kleshas, birth and death, and freedom from those is a good way to feel

Here Milarepa describes the nature of genuine reality in a way that is in harmony with how the Buddha taught in the second turning of the wheel of Dharma. For example, *The Heart Sutra* says: "There is no ignorance nor any ending of ignorance, no aging and death nor any ending of aging and death, and nothing in between."

Birth, aging, and death are only confused appearances. For example, we can have a dream of getting sick and dying, but these appearances are only confused thoughts and perceptions because in the true nature of the dream there is no sickness or death at all. Similarly, although birth and death appear, in the true nature of reality there is no birth and no death at all. The true nature of reality, which transcends kleshas (disturbing emotions), birth, and death, is open, spacious, and relaxed.

Then what are kleshas, birth, aging, and death? They are not real at all. They are just the confusion of thoughts that do not know the true nature of reality.

As Milarepa sang in another song, *The Three Kinds of Confidence in Genuine Reality:*

I've gained confidence that there is no arising
This swept away my taking past and future lives as two
Exposed all six realms' appearances as false
And cut right through believing all too much in birth and death

I've gained confidence in everything as equal
This swept away my taking happiness and grief as two
Exposed the ups and downs of feelings as false
And cut believing there are some to have and some to shun

In inseparability I've gained confidence
This swept away samsara and nirvana seen as two
Exposed the exercise of paths and levels as false
And cut right through believing all too much in hope and fear*

This is Milarepa's warrior song, which is sung in a melody and style of the American heroes—the cowboys. So when you sing this song, ride your horse like the Khampa cowboys of eastern Tibet. Hold the

---

* This song was translated under the guidance of Khenpo Tsültrim Gyamtso Rinpoche by Jim Scott in 1998. The original Tibetan source is *Mi la ras pa'i rnam mgur* (n.p.: mtsho sngon mi rigs dpe skrun khang, 1989), p. 298.

reins in your left hand and a horse whip in your right hand. At the end of each verse, whoop like a cowboy!

The point of shouting like that is that when you sing loudly, in the strongest voice that you can, your mind enters a state of complete nonconceptuality. You become a warrior.

It is like when practicing Chö, you shout a loud "*peht*" that cuts through coarse concepts, and then you let your mind rest in its nonconceptual true nature.

BULLIES ARE GOOD

With the bullies getting worse and worse, I feel extremely well

When you stay overnight in charnel grounds, and you are actually confronted by fearsome and nasty demons, what is that like? It is even better than before. Not only is it fantastic, but it is better than anything that has happened before.

Sometimes, when Milarepa was meditating in a cave, a fearsome demon or demons would come and try to scare or hurt him. But Milarepa meditated on these demons' true nature, and so instead of harming him, the demons became the friends of his meditation. They even became his students.

Whatever harm demons or other bullies do to you, whatever suffering they cause, if you can simply rest in equipoise, and realize that all these appearances of negativity are actually luminous clarity's own energy and play, then as a result of the appearances of negativity your experience of ease, relaxation, and bliss will be even greater than before. So the more you realize suffering and negativity's true nature, the happier you will be.

Negativity can be directed at us from different directions: from our enemies, friends, those who we do not really know well at all, and even from our own minds when we get angry. The point of our practice is to recognize that the basic nature of all this negativity is the inherent peace and openness that is the true nature of mind. Then, whatever negativity we experience, it does not harm us; it helps us. It is a friend of our meditation.

One example of how to meditate on the essential nature of negativity, particularly that of anger, is found in the story of Amka Sembewa. He was a yogi who lived together with his yogini consort, their children, and their goats in a mountain cave in Nangchen Jobrah, near where I am from in Kham, in Eastern Tibet. This yogi and yogini were an extraordinary couple, because whenever they were visited by their sponsors—the people who brought them food and other gifts—they were always found fighting. They fought ferociously, by shouting and calling each other all kinds of derogatory names.

Once, in front of their sponsors they fought so ferociously that the yogini ran up to the top of a peak and yelled, "I hate you so much I am going to jump!" And from down below, Amka Sembewa replied, "Jump! Jump!" But she did not jump; instead she came back down and fought with him more! Then one night they fought so loudly that all night long they could be heard in the village below their cave, and even as far as three mountains away. In the morning, however, people saw rainbows above their cave, and when they went up to the cave there was nothing left of them at all—they had attained the rainbow body. This was because what they were actually doing all along was meditating on anger's essential nature. Thus, if we are able to meditate on anger and other negativity's essential nature, that can become one of the most profound and powerful meditations of all.

SICKNESS AND HEALTH ARE EQUALLY GOOD

When there's not a painful illness in sight, feels even better still

If there is an illness, that is good. It is not a problem. And if there is no illness, that is not something to feel bad about—that is also good! It is good to be healthy.

If we only talked about sickness and difficulty being good, then some people might try to make themselves sick and make things hard for themselves. But there is no need to do that, because being healthy and having things go well for you are also good.

Suffering Is Bliss

The suffering being bliss feels so good that feeling bad feels good

What is suffering like? Suffering's true nature is emptiness; emptiness's true nature is luminous clarity; and luminous clarity's true nature is bliss. Therefore, suffering's true nature is bliss.

The good thing about suffering is that there is no distraction from it. When you suffer and then meditate, there is no chance of being distracted to something else, because your suffering holds your attention completely. So you have no choice but to realize the suffering's true nature.

To do this, analyze suffering in the same way that I described how to analyze mind itself, and then how to analyze fear. Look directly at the thought of suffering in your mind and ask: "Does this thought of suffering have any shape or color? When I look at this thought of suffering, do I see it anywhere in my body or outside of it? Where did the suffering in my mind come from? Where is it now? Where will it go? Does it arise or cease?"

Do this analysis precisely. For example, try to find the exact place where the suffering in your mind arose. Try to locate its origin, and where it is now. After it is gone, locate the place where it went. When we examine suffering in this way, we cannot find any of these.

Once you know that the suffering is empty, the next step is to relax within your certainty in this. When you do, your mind is naturally luminous, clear, and blissful, because that has been the basic nature of the suffering all along.

Natural Exercise and Dance Feels Good

Since the trulkhor comes from what I am, it feels extremely good

Trulkhor is the term for physical yogic exercise that is taught in the Vajrayana. In Hindu teachings as well there are many physical yogic techniques. However, all these formal Buddhist and non-Buddhist exercises are specifically regulated. There are many different movements that you have to learn how to do.

It is much nicer to let mind rest in its natural state and to let bodily movement flow naturally from that. That kind of exercise feels great, and that is what Milarepa is describing here. When you move your body while resting in mind's basic nature, then all physical movement flows from that. Every movement of body becomes natural trulkhor yoga, which feels very good.

For example, move your hand and fingers and let mind rest in its own basic state while you do. That is yogic exercise. Similarly, all movements of the body are trulkhor yoga when mind is resting in its own nature and you are just letting the body move naturally. Profound yoga comes when mind is resting in its own nature.

Sometimes when you move your body, look at the essential nature of the feelings that arise, and rest in their true nature. It does not matter what you are feeling—it could be pleasurable, painful, or neutral. The essential nature of all these feelings is the same, and this is what we need to realize.

In this kind of yogic exercise there are no rules. You can move your body any way you want to. Any way that feels good and natural, just move like that, and see what different kinds of experiences arise when you do. Rest your mind in its natural state, breathe easily, and relax. Move your body in a natural way, and see what happens.

To leap and run about is dance—feels even better still

How is it when you just dance and jump around? Even better! Milarepa stayed all alone in his caves, and sometimes he would go out and run, leap, and dance around. In Buddhism and other traditions there are formal types of dance that have structure and rules about how you have to move and at what time. But Milarepa's way of leaping and dancing transcends all rules and forms. It is natural dance, and so it is quite wonderful.

When we do other kinds of dance and exercise that have rules and ways that we are supposed to do them, then we are prone to think: "I am not doing it right. I should not do it this way, I should do it better." Sometimes we might think, "Now I am really doing it right." We have all these thoughts of contrivance. But when we just move naturally, those thoughts do not arise. We can just let them all go, and relax.

Milarepa's running, leaping, and dancing about are connected with the profound view and meditation, which is why all his movements are experiences of bliss. If while you move, you do not have the profound view of the true nature of reality, and do not rest in meditation within that, bliss will not arise. That is why the profound view and meditation are important.

Singing Feels Good

To be a king of speech with a treasury of song feels good

What is Milarepa's speech like? He is a king of speech, which means that he is able to spontaneously sing songs of realization. When you can do that, then without forethought or contrivance, Dharma teaching is a natural expression of your speech. It is like having a treasure chest of Dharma songs always at your disposal, and that feels good.

Milarepa is also a king of speech because his songs are naturally and immediately triumphant, effortless, and joyful. He does not need to think to himself: "Now I have to sing a song that will make me happy." He does not have to put that kind of effort into it. The way he sings naturally makes him happy.

The sound of a song is sound-emptiness. Mind rests relaxed, free from contrivance. And the song's subject is equality. When that is the case, everything is wonderful, and Milarepa sang an immeasurable number of this kind of spontaneous Dharma song.

That the words are like the buzzing of bees feels extremely good

This refers to the beautiful sound bumblebees make when they fly around flowers. Milarepa's songs were naturally beautiful, so much so that even animals loved to listen to him sing.

Also, since the buzzing of bees is a quiet and peaceful sound, Milarepa is teaching here that one does not necessarily need to sing in a loud voice in order to sing well. Some people think that they always need to sing loudly, but that is not correct. The happiness that comes from singing songs of realization does not depend on whether you sing loudly or softly. Sometimes it is nice to sing in a loud voice, and sometimes to sing in a soft voice. The key point is while you sing, let your mind rest in its basic nature, luminous and relaxed.

That the sound it makes is merit collecting feels even better still

When you sing while resting within the realization of sound-emptiness, whatever you sing is meritorious. And the more you sing, the more merit you accumulate. Knowing that makes the experience even better.

Songs do not arise from just one cause or condition; rather, they require a collection of causes and conditions. To make a sound in a song, you need your vocal chords, tongue, the roof of your mouth, and lips; and all of these have to be working in precisely the right way. Furthermore, for there to be a sound there also needs to be an ear to hear it, an ear-sense-consciousness to perceive it, and a thought: "I hear a sound." Thus, sound is produced by the coming together of many causes and conditions, and therefore it is a dependently arisen mere appearance that does not have any inherent nature.

The mahasiddha Tilopa gave some advice to a singer on how to meditate:

When you are sad, look at the city of gandharvas,
When you listen, listen to the bees' song,
When you look, look with the eyes of one blind since birth,
All you hear is like an echo.

"Look at the city of gandharvas" means to look at appearances knowing they are appearance-emptiness. "Listen to the bees' song" means to listen to sounds knowing they are sound-emptiness. Bees' sounds are sound-emptiness, and also we do not get so fixated on the sounds that bees make, so the instruction is to listen to sounds while at the same time being aware of their true nature and not fixating on them. "Look with the eyes of one blind since birth" means to look with your eye of wisdom at the true nature of reality, originally free from any reference point. Look at it in a nondual way, free from there being anything to see and anyone seeing anything. Then, "all you hear is like an echo"—you realize that all the pleasant and unpleasant sounds you hear are equally sound-emptiness, like echoes and sounds in dreams.

When we follow this advice, singing, dancing, and making music become a profound meditation practice.

The mahasiddha Saraha was a dancer. He would meditate while he was dancing, and that again was a most profound practice. If you connect singing and dancing with the profound view and meditation, every time you sing and dance, it is Dharma practice.

Mind's Natural Qualities and Bliss

The bliss is good in the expanse of the confidence of strength
of mind

The mind's natural qualities are strength, power, brilliant clarity, courage, and confidence. Where are these qualities? In the bliss of the expanse that is mind's basic state.

The reason why these qualities are naturally present in mind is that mind itself is clarity-emptiness, beyond dualistic reference point. For if a quality like courage has a reference point that we think is truly existent—if we think we are courageous with regard to something or about something—if we reify it like that, it is destined to disintegrate. It can never last. It is not true courage. True courage is in the bliss that is present in the expanse of mind itself, free of dualistic clinging.

What develops on its own by its own force feels extremely good

The bliss that arises is natural bliss. It is spontaneously present, meaning that you do not need to try to create it. It is already there.

You do not need to try to make yourself happy, because the true nature of your mind is already happy. When we are only able to make ourselves happy by putting a lot of effort into it, that type of happiness is tenuous and will fade quickly. Happiness that comes as a result of attachment to outer things is in fact reduced by that attachment, and it will turn into suffering. In contrast, this bliss is free from attachment, clinging, and fixation. The experience of the natural bliss that exists inherently in mind itself is most wonderful.

What comes out looking like a hodgepodge feels even better still

Knowing this, there can be all different kinds of experiences—it does not matter! A wide variety of experience is even better.

If you dream and do not know you are dreaming, then when different things happen in the dream, you like some of them and do not like others. But that is not because there is any actual difference between the appearances; it only happens because of the confusion that does not recognize the dream. But if you dream and know you are dreaming, then whatever different appearances manifest, they are all the experience of bliss. There can appear to be a friend or an enemy—they are both equally of the nature of bliss.

A Parting Gift

This happy experience song by a yogi carefree
Is for you who believe in what you're doing here
To take along with you when you go

Milarepa's students have come to meet him, and he has given them this song as a present to take with them when they part. It is like when you go to a party, the hosts might give you a little gift to take home with you. Milarepa did not have any material possessions, so he gave his students the gifts of his songs of realization. What wonderful gifts they are—we are still enjoying them today.

Questions and Answers

Question: Could you please explain more about how to look at the true nature of mind?

Khenpo Tsültrim Gyamtso Rinpoche: Look at the true nature of mind in a way that transcends there being anything to look at and anyone looking. Then you will see mind's nature in a way that transcends there being anything to see and anyone seeing.

For as long as there is something to look at and someone looking, your mode of looking will be conceptual. And since concepts constantly change, so the way you look and what you see will constantly change. If you look at mind and see something—good or bad, superior or inferior—whatever you see is just your own conceptual projection. In fact, mind's true nature transcends concepts and duality, so you cannot look at it in any conceptual or dualistic way. When you are able to "look" at mind in a way that transcends the concepts of looker and looked upon, in relative reality that is called "seeing" the true nature of mind.

Milarepa sang, "When there is nothing to look at, that is supreme seeing." When there is something to look at, that is not the best view. The best view is when there's nothing conceivable to look at.

This is why it is taught: "Look and do not find; rest within clarity." When you analyze mind you cannot find it; not finding anything, when you let mind settle naturally, it is clear and brilliant. The first part of this instruction is in harmony with the middle turning of the wheel; the second part in harmony with the final turning; and when you put them together, you have a profound pith instruction of Mahamudra and Dzogchen.

Q: If bliss is spontaneously present, why is it so difficult to find?

KTGR: "Spontaneously present" and "not spontaneously present" are conceptual fabrications. They exist in dependence upon the thoughts of the individuals who are thinking about them. It is the same with "difficult" and "easy." So if you think something is difficult, then for you it is difficult, whereas for someone else it may seem easy because they think it is easy. It is only difficult or easy because you think it is. The true nature of reality transcends all conceptual fabrications.

Part Three

Mahayana Aspiration Prayers

6

Transform the Present, Brighten the Future, Light Up the Universe

AN OVERVIEW BY ROSE TAYLOR

KHENPO RINPOCHE emphasizes the importance of aspiration prayers in our Dharma practice. Rinpoche explains that according to the Mahayana teachings, the ability to benefit others is a factor of mind, and therefore this ability is something that we can develop until it becomes limitless. The way to do this is to make aspiration prayers that we may be of increasing benefit to others.

As ordinary beings, we may wonder how we can truly benefit others. Sometimes it is possible to alleviate people's suffering directly, and we should do that. But we may regularly see a lot of suffering in the course of our daily lives, work, and relationships. We constantly come into contact with sentient beings' suffering whenever we watch the news on television or read newspapers. It can seem that the suffering in samsara is overwhelming and that we are powerless in the face of so many problems. But this is precisely where making altruistic aspiration prayers can be so effective. Altruistic aspiration prayers are a skillful way to make the present more positive and to be of deeper benefit in the long term.

Buddha Nature: The Source of Aspiration Prayers' Power

In the practice of making aspiration prayers, the first step is to recognize that the actual essence of mind is the stainless buddha nature. Because of this, we have a powerful inherent ability to transform the impure world we perceive into a pure one. We do this by working with mind.

We can work with mind in all circumstances. Even at times when we feel that we cannot help others because we are tired, sick, or lack material resources, we always have the ability to make aspiration prayers for others' happiness, and for us to be able to be of future benefit to those who suffer.

In fact, when we ourselves suffer, although we may feel inadequate, we actually have even more ability to help others because we can empathize that much more with their suffering. We can always resolve to engender positive change and aspire to gather material resources and skill in order to benefit others. Thus, we come to see that no situation is hopeless when we make altruistic aspiration prayers.

We can even work with the situation of death in this way. The worldly way of thinking is that death breaks our connection with the deceased, so we cannot help them any longer. But since the Middle Way teaches that birth and death are not truly existent, death does not truly separate us from the ones we love. So we can still make aspiration prayers for them and pray that we will meet them again and again in ever-improving circumstances. Making similar prayers with regard to our Dharma teachers is also how we can ensure that we will meet our teachers lifetime after lifetime and continue our Dharma practice under their guidance.

Even when we see a tragic event on the news in which many people have died, we can use that connection with the deceased to pray that their next set of circumstances improve, that they find happiness, and that we can be of benefit to them.

COMBINING ALTRUISTIC ACTIVITY WITH WISDOM

Rinpoche teaches that when we are making aspiration prayers or performing other types of altruistic activity, it is important to mix this activity with wisdom realizing emptiness. When we engage in altruistic activity without understanding emptiness, we run into all kinds of problems—if we are successful in benefiting others we become arrogant, and if we are unsuccessful we become discouraged. That is why it is important to cultivate our wisdom realizing that self and other are not truly existent. If we meditate on how it is that the one who is performing benefit does not truly exist and the ones who are being benefited do not truly exist, we gain freedom from arrogance and despair, from hope and fear.

We can develop such wisdom by asking ourselves, "Am I benefiting others like in a dream when I know I am dreaming? What is the nature of the ones I am benefiting and of myself as the one being of benefit?" Most important, we can ask, "What is the essence of this mind that is thinking of benefiting others?" Then, making aspiration prayers becomes a method for realizing mind's true nature.

ASPIRATION PRAYERS' TRANSFORMATIVE POWER

Making altruistic aspiration prayers in this way, we transform our present state of mind. Simply switching from our continual preoccupation with ourselves to focusing on others is an important transformation in itself. But we can also transform difficult situations that feel solid and stuck by using aspiration prayers to develop a basic sense of goodness in our connections with others. For example, we may have difficult relationships with certain people. Perhaps we feel deeply hurt by someone and unable to approach them directly. But we can still maintain the positive aspiration that in the future our relationship with them will improve, that we will be able to be of benefit to them, and that they will find lasting happiness. In other relationships, where perhaps we feel that we did not do enough for someone we are now separated from, or else there is someone we wish we could benefit more but we do not immediately see how to do so, we can make aspiration prayers for them and thereby keep our connection with them positive.

THE BUDDHA'S EXAMPLE

The Buddha Shakyamuni gives us an excellent and inspirational example of how to keep this ground of goodness in relationships, even those with very difficult and mean-spirited people. The Buddha had a particularly difficult relationship with his cousin Devadatta, who was jealous of the Buddha's good qualities and wide acclaim as a teacher. Devadatta tried various means to discredit the Buddha, turn his students against him, and even to kill him.

Rather than making the Buddha angry, however, Devadatta only evoked his compassion. Once a student asked the Buddha why he tolerated Devadatta, instead of using his miraculous powers to put an end to Devadatta's mischief once and for all. The Buddha replied that in fact he had known Devadatta in many previous lifetimes, and Devadatta had continually behaved in the same malicious way. However, by doing so Devadatta had actually assisted the Buddha's progress to enlightenment by providing the conditions for him to practice patience. So, the Buddha felt no malice toward his cousin, only gratitude and love.

Toward the end of Devadatta's life, he was afflicted with remorse. He called out to the Buddha for help and, due to the power of the connection between his giving rise to faith and the Buddha's compassion toward him, in his future lifetimes he became an excellent Dharma practitioner. Because the Buddha never rejected Devadatta, their relationship was never severed and the Buddha was there to help Devadatta when he was ready to accept it.

Modern Buddhist masters also give us clear examples of the power of training in compassion and aspiration prayers. To be in the presence of such masters is to feel their compassion, joy, and inner peace, and to experience joy and inner peace ourselves as a result. At the same time, our teachers often remind us that they are not supernatural, but rather are human beings just like ourselves. Therefore, we have the potential to develop the same qualities and ability to benefit others that we so admire in them. Making aspiration prayers with altruistic motivation brings us joy and inner peace, which has a positive effect certainly for ourselves and also for those who come into contact with us.

Thus, by dissolving our ego fixation, thinking altruistically, and making aspiration prayers, we can transform whatever circumstances occur into highly positive ones, and lay the ground for ever-improving situations in the future. In this way, we light up the universe with auspicious connections in the present and for the future.

How to Practice with Aspiration Prayers

When making aspiration prayers, you can use the ones in this book, those composed by other masters, and your own original prayers. It is good to make up your own prayers to fit the particular situations you encounter. Rinpoche teaches that you can sing or recite these prayers at any time, silently or out loud. When you do, connect with your heart's true wish that all beings be free of suffering and enjoy great happiness. Think how wonderful it would be if that were to happen not just for your own family and friends, but for those you dislike and those you do not know at all.

Then, let go of thoughts and let mind rest in its basic nature, luminous clarity. After a few moments, imagine that the sky around you is filled with the buddhas and bodhisattvas of the ten directions. They are there to witness you set the intention to benefit all beings in both temporary and ultimate ways. Doing this helps to remind you that you are not acting in isolation, because you are invoking the wisdom, compassion, and enlightened activity of all the buddhas and bodhisattvas. That is a skillful method which gives your prayer more power and energy. Then recite the prayer, and when you have finished, again briefly rest the mind in its true nature beyond reference point.

7

A Prayer That These True Words Be Swiftly Fulfilled

TRANSLATED BY ROSE TAYLOR

Translator's Note

Exemplifying the way that aspiration prayers can be made anywhere, at any time, Khenpo Rinpoche composed A Prayer That These True Words Be Swiftly Fulfilled *on a plane trip from Bangkok to India. It was the last international flight of his 1998 round-the-world teaching tour, and he spontaneously sang this prayer as a way to dedicate the merit of his efforts to the benefit of everyone. In April 2007, when Rinpoche arrived in Seattle from Nepal for an extended stay, he asked that a melody be made for this prayer and that his students sing it many times.*

To the victorious ones of ten directions and their heirs,
To the mother of the fourfold nobles, Mother Dharmakaya,
To the one who performs the buddhas' deeds, Lady Tara,
With my three doors* I prostrate with great respect.

May all beings in existence be free from the lower realms' suffering
By attaining the excellent support of the higher realms

* Body, speech, and mind.

And may they progress on the path of three vehicles,*
And thus achieve unsurpassable, perfect enlightenment!

Here in this world, may fear arising from four elements,**
The fear of war, sickness, famine, and other harm—
All adverse conditions be completely pacified,
And may good conditions, Dharma and prosperity, flourish!

When the affluent gather, guard, and increase their wealth,
May they not suffer because of their fortune.
May they benefit the destitute, sick, and tormented,
And thus boldly transform wealth to mountains of merit!

May the poor be free of such suffering
As the constant lack of food, clothes, and shelter,
And when they find these, may conflict not increase—
May material enjoyments embellish their joy!

May the mighty and powerful be free
Of the suffering of ruin, and harm caused by jealousy.
May they be free of all harmful conditions,
And may they use their good fortune to benefit others!

May the weak no longer be powerless,
May they be free of illness and calamity.
May they be free of all the pain of the oppressed,
Enjoying happiness like the gods' abundance!

May all those who suffer in relation to me—
My enemies who suffer because of anger,
And my friends who suffer due to attachment—
May they realize that all is equality!

---

* The vehicles of the hearers, of the solitary realizers, and of the bodhisattvas (also known as the Mahayana).
** Earth, water, fire, and wind. Disturbances in these four elements bring the danger of physical sickness and natural disasters.

In short, with my body, speech, and mind
May I not do the slightest harm to anyone,
May I lead whomever I meet to the authentic path,
In all my lifetimes may I benefit others!

By the buddhas' and bodhisattvas' compassion,
Reality's clear light, fabrication-free,
And seeming reality's unerring causes and results,
May all of these aspirations be swiftly fulfilled!

COLOPHON

On the sky-path above the Indian Ocean on the way from Thailand, this was spoken extemporaneously by Sherab Lodrö, December 14, 1998.*

---

* Khenpo Rinpoche went by the name "Sherab Lodrö" as a young boy.

8

Auspiciousness That Lights Up the Universe

TRANSLATED BY ARI GOLDFIELD

Translator's Note

Rinpoche composed Auspiciousness That Lights Up the Universe *on a beautiful morning in Kathmandu, Nepal, in December 1997. After extemporaneously singing this prayer, he spent the whole day touring the Kathmandu Valley with Chime Dorje and Tsepak Dorje, two of his Tibetan attendants, and me. We visited many sacred places, stupas, monasteries, and temples, and sang* Auspiciousness That Lights Up the Universe *again and again. Since then Rinpoche regularly had his students sing this prayer at the end of his teaching sessions. Once he even offered it via fax to His Holiness the Seventeenth Gyalwang Karmapa.*

NAMO GURU HASA VAJRA YE!*
You see that everything in samsara and nirvana
Is merely dependently arisen
You see the Dharmata, the true being

---

* "I prostrate to the guru, Shepa Dorje." "Shepa Dorje" is the name that Milarepa was given simultaneously by Marpa and the deities in the mandala of Chakrasamvara, one of the main Vajrayana deities practiced in the Kagyu lineage.

That is the essence of all dependent arising
The power of your great insight
Fills the universe with auspicious light
Oh mighty Shepa Dorje
Please rise up now from within my heart.

Ground's basic nature transcends conceptuality
And like water-moons, appearances arise dependently
May everyone realize that this is true
And dispel the darkness cast by doubt and wrong view
And may their realization's auspiciousness
Light up the whole universe!

The vision of your wisdom is amazing*
You see just how things are, you see everything
As parents love their children, so you love all beings
You bring us benefit and happiness
Your power makes disciples out of your enemies—
May your auspiciousness light up the universe!

For samsara's cause, clinging to "I" and "me,"
The Dharma realizing selflessness is the greatest remedy
May all beings use it to pacify
Their confused belief that there is an "I"
And by the power of this great happening
May auspiciousness light up the universe!

The ways of ordinary beings, you have left behind—
Noble ones who realize reality, the true nature of mind**
May you lead all ordinary beings
Who have not yet entered, to the path of peace

* This verse's supplication is addressed to the Buddha.
** This verse is addressed to the noble bodhisattvas—"noble" because they have directly realized the true nature of reality, a realization that they will bring to perfection when they attain the state of buddhahood.

And by this may auspiciousness
Light up the whole universe!

May the yidams who bestow the siddhis
And the protectors who clear obstacles away
Eliminate all harmful conditions—
Everything adverse to the path
And by this may auspiciousness
Light up the whole universe!

May the noble path of nonviolence
Flourish in all the worlds there are
When beings meet and interact
May the connections they make be filled with love
And by this may auspiciousness
Light up the whole universe!

During this twenty-first century
That is one of such prosperity
May struggle over wealth and gain
Disappear and not be seen again
Free from strife and violence
May all enjoy great abundance
And by this may auspiciousness
Light up the whole universe!

During this twenty-first century
When science is advancing incredibly
Amazing and wondrous, these new machines
That bring the gods' enjoyments to human beings
May they be used with skill supreme
To end violence and cause peace to reign
And by this may auspiciousness
Light up the whole universe!

May the sciences that explore outside
Be joined with the inner science of the mind
To excellently put an end
To mistaken views and confusion
And by this may auspiciousness
Light up the whole universe!

The source of all this auspiciousness
Is the true nature of mind, so luminous!
So may realization of mind, just as it is
Set the universe ablaze with auspicious excellence!

Through all of this auspiciousness
Wherever its light may be seen
With the love and the compassion
That make bodhichitta mind supreme
May this thought arise in everyone:
"Other beings' happiness is as important as my own"
And may excellent virtue and auspiciousness
Always increase, never diminish!

Colophon

On December 28, 1997, in the Garden of Translation near the Great
Stupa of Boudhanath, Nepal, this was spoken extemporaneously by
the one only called "Khenpo," Tsültrim Gyamtso.

Acknowledgments

THERE ARE COUNTLESS PEOPLE whose devotion and friendship have supported Khenpo Tsültrim Gyamtso Rinpoche and ourselves while Rinpoche has been in semi-retreat these past few years, and our deep gratitude goes out to all of them. In particular, we would like to thank those who lent their valued help to bringing this book to publication: Emily Bower, our expert editor, and the rest of the skillful staff of Shambhala Publications, including Ben Gleason, assistant editor, and Hazel Bercholz, art director, and Jim Zaccaria, cover designer. We also wish to thank Sarah Whitehorn for her transcription work of Khenpo Rinpoche's teaching that forms the basis of "The Path of Faith and the Path of Reasoning"; and Acharya Tashi Wangchuk and Tsepak Dorje for answering questions about the Tibetan recordings of Khenpo Rinpoche's teachings on *The Stages of View at the Heart of Definitive Meaning*.

Glossary

AGGREGATES (Skt.: *skandhas*)   The five classifications that comprise all material and mental phenomena: forms, feelings, discriminations, formations, and consciousnesses. Each individual sentient being's existence is imputed in dependence upon their own unique collection of these aggregates, but this is a dependently arisen mere appearance. The problem arises when an individual believes that their aggregates somehow constitute a truly existent self. Therefore, the Buddha taught the methods of how to examine the aggregates and see that there is no truly existent self to be found in the aggregates' multitude of constantly changing, dependently existent parts. See also Selflessness of the individual.

ALL-BASE CONSCIOUSNESS   *See* Base-consciousness.

AMKA SEMBEWA   A Tibetan yogi who, together with his yogini consort, gained realization by meditating on anger's true nature.

ARHAT   A practitioner who has attained the fruition of either the vehicle of the hearers or the solitary realizers. By cultivating strong revulsion for and renunciation of samsara, and by perfecting their realization of the selflessness of the individual, the arhats completely free themselves from the disturbing emotions and gain liberation from samsara. At a certain point, however, the buddhas wake them up from the peace of their meditative state, reveal to them that they have not yet attained the fruition of buddhahood itself, and exhort them to practice the Mahayana teachings for the benefit of all sentient beings. Doing so, they eventually attain the complete and perfect enlightenment of the buddhas.

ARYADEVA (second to third century C.E.)   A renowned student of
Nagarjuna. He composed many texts to explain Nagarjuna's teachings,
including most famously *The Four Hundred Stanzas on the Middle Way.*

AUTONOMY SCHOOL (Skt.: *Svatantrika Madhyamaka*)   One of two
branches of the Empty-of-Self Middle Way school. Its followers refute
true existence and assert that emptiness is the true nature of reality.

BARDO   "Intermediate state." The time when a sentient being's
consciousness is between the end of one lifetime and the beginning
of the next.

BASE-CONSCIOUSNESS (Skt.: *alaya-vijnana*)   The subtle aspect of
mind that is the basis or support of all mental activity. It is also the
repository of an individual's habitual patterns of perception, thought,
emotion, and action. This term is also translated as "all-base consciousness."

BODHICHITTA   "Awakening mind." Bodhichitta has two aspects.
Relative bodhichitta, arising from the cultivation of all-embracing
love and compassion, is the commitment to lead all sentient beings
to the state of the complete and perfect enlightenment of buddhahood. Ultimate bodhichitta is the true nature of reality itself. In
Mahayana Buddhist practice, one cultivates and meditates on both
types of bodhichitta.

BODHISATTVA   "Courageous one of enlightenment." A follower of
the Mahayana path who cultivates the two types of bodhichitta.
There are both ordinary bodhisattvas and noble bodhisattvas, the
latter distinguished by their direct realization of the true nature of
reality. Bodhisattvas are courageous because they take the vow to stay
in samsara in order to benefit sentient beings, rather than seeking to
escape from it. When bodhisattvas bring their wisdom and compassion to perfection, they become buddhas.

BUDDHA   The teacher; an individual who has attained enlightenment by perfecting wisdom that realizes the true nature of reality
and compassion for all sentient beings. Shakyamuni, originally Prince

Gautama, is the original buddha of our era who gave the founding Buddhist teachings in this world; however, the Mahayana teaches that countless sentient beings have and will achieve buddhahood.

BUDDHA NATURE (Skt.: *sugata-garbha* or *tathagata-garbha*)   The true nature of mind—wisdom that is inherently pure and naturally endowed with the qualities of enlightenment. Thus, to attain enlightenment is not to construct something anew or to acquire something that one does not already possess; rather it is to realize one's own basic nature and potential.

CHANDRAKIRTI (sixth to seventh century)   Indian master and exponent of the Middle Way Consequence school, most famously in his commentary called *Entering the Middle Way,* which explains the meaning of *The Fundamental Wisdom of the Middle Way.*

CHÖ   "Cutting through." In this practice, one trains in generosity and fearlessness by going to frightening places and visualizing offering one's body to demons and other "guests." It was initially taught by the incomparable Tibetan yogini Machik Labdrön (1055–1153), who gained her realization as a result of studying *The Transcendent Wisdom Sutras* of the second turning of the wheel of Dharma.

CITY OF GANDHARVAS   See Gandharvas.

CLARITY-EMPTINESS   See Luminosity-emptiness.

CONCEPTUAL FABRICATIONS   All the labels that thoughts fabricate and cling to as accurate descriptions of the things that thoughts believe to exist. They are countless in number, but examples are: "good," "bad," "person," "object," "pleasure," "pain," "you," "me," "hot," and "cold." When phenomena and mind are described as being beyond fabrication in their true nature, that means that their true nature transcends all thoughts we might have about what it might be; it is inexpressible and inconceivable.

CONSEQUENCE SCHOOL (Skt.: *Prasangika Madhyamaka*)   One of two branches of the Empty-of-Self Middle Way school. Its followers refute true existence but do not assert that the true nature of reality is emptiness or anything else, because they realize that since genuine reality transcends all conceptual fabrications, to make an assertion about it would obscure the realization of its inconceivable essence.

DEFINITIVE MEANING   The teachings on genuine reality, empty of the self; empty of duality; free from arising, abiding, and ceasing; transcending conceptual fabrication; by nature luminous clarity, bliss-emptiness, and awareness-emptiness.

DEMIGOD   See Six realms.

DEPENDENTLY ARISEN MERE APPEARANCES   The essential quality of all possible appearances. Whatever it is that appears, it can only do so in dependence upon its causes and conditions, and so it is a mere appearance, empty of any nature of its own. The classic example is the moon that appears on the surface of a pool of water.

DEVADATTA   The Buddha Shakyamuni's cousin, who, although he possessed many outstanding physical and mental qualities, was jealous of the Buddha and tried many ways to harm him and his teachings. The Buddha never gave up on him, and in the end he became an outstanding Dharma practitioner.

DHARMA   Refers to phenomena in general, and in particular to the phenomenon of Buddhist teachings.

DHARMAKAYA   A dimension of the buddhas' enlightenment; a dimension of the true nature of mind; and a synonym for genuine reality. Also called the "mother" of the four types of noble beings—hearers, solitary realizers, bodhisattvas, and buddhas—because it is by gaining realization of Dharmakaya to the various degrees they do that these noble beings attain their status. See also Three kayas.

DHARMATA   "Essential reality." A synonym of "genuine reality" and "the true nature of reality." Whereas *dharma* is any particular phenomenon, *Dharmata* is that phenomenon's essential nature.

DOLPOPA SHERAB GYALTSEN (1292–1361)   A great Tibetan master and proponent of the Empty-of-Other school, he wrote *Mountain Retreat Teachings: The Ocean of Definitive Meaning*, among other texts, to explain that school's teachings and defend them as teachings of definitive meaning.

DZOGCHEN   "The great completion." A profound set of instructions that describe the true nature of reality as awareness-emptiness and that explain how to meditate upon this true nature.

EIGHT CONSCIOUSNESSES   The five sense consciousnesses; the mental consciousness; the afflicted consciousness (the aspect of mind that is unaware of its true nature, and that believes that the self and phenomena truly exist); and the base-consciousness.

EMPTINESS OF PHENOMENA   The abiding reality of all phenomena, which is that they are empty of inherent nature, and ultimately empty of any conceptual notion of what they might be, even the notion of emptiness itself.

EMPTY-OF-OTHER SCHOOL (Tib.: *shen-tong*)   The branch of the Middle Way whose explanations are based on the Buddha's teachings from the third turning of the wheel of Dharma. This school's name derives from the explanation that the true nature of mind, the buddha nature, is empty of that which is different from or "other" to it, namely conceptual fabrications and the adventitious stains of suffering and confusion; but is not empty of its own natural qualities, which include awareness, clarity, and bliss.

EMPTY-OF-SELF SCHOOL (Tib.: *rang-tong*)   The branch of the Middle Way whose explanations are based on the Buddha's teachings from the second turning of the wheel of Dharma. It is composed of the Middle Way Autonomy and Middle Way Consequence schools. Its name derives from the explanation that all outer and inner phenomena are empty of their own essence—they are empty of whatever it is that they appear to be. For example, "Anger is empty of anger" would be a statement this school would make, because when one subjects anger or any other phenomenon to logical analysis, the phenomenon cannot be found.

EQUALITY Contradictions, opposites, differences, and distinctions appear but do not truly exist. In genuine reality, opposites, differences, and distinctions are undifferentiable; they all have the same basic nature.

GAMPOPA (1079–1153) Of Milarepa's twenty-five great disciples, Gampopa was "like the sun." He is the author of *The Ornament of Precious Liberation*, the famous comprehensive text on the stages of the Buddhist path.

GANDHARVAS A type of spirit that lives together with others of its kind in large communities. When looked at from far away it seems as if there is a whole city of them, but when approached they seem to vanish. This is why "city of gandharvas" is one of the examples the Buddha gave for how things could appear while not truly existing.

GENUINE REALITY Neither an object of the sense consciousnesses nor conceivable by thoughts, it is the true nature of all consciousnesses and their objects. It can be ascertained through analysis and experienced in meditation. When its experience becomes direct realization, one becomes a noble bodhisattva; when this direct realization is perfected, one becomes a noble buddha.

GOTSANGPA (1189–1258) An emanation of Milarepa and a great early master of the Drukpa Kagyu lineage, he came four generations after Gampopa.

HEART SUTRA Perhaps the most famous of *The Transcendent Wisdom Sutras* (Skt.: *Prajnaparamita Sutras*) that constitute the second turning of the wheel of Dharma, this concise teaching comes in the form of a dialogue between the Buddha's disciple Shariputra and the great bodhisattva Avalokiteshvara (Tib.: *Chenrezik*). The sutra teaches that all phenomena are of the nature of emptiness, and that all the buddhas and bodhisattvas rely on the transcendent wisdom that realizes this emptiness. It is considered to be the speech of the Buddha because it was spoken in the Buddha's presence and with the power of his blessing.

HELL BEING   See Six realms.

HUNGRY GHOST   See Six realms.

ILLUSION-LIKE SAMADHI   *Samadhi* refers to a state in which one is concentrated and not distracted. Paradoxically, it seems, the illusion-like samadhi is the meditation one practices in the times between formal meditation sessions, in the midst of all the distractions of thoughts and the objects that appear to the senses. When one remembers that all of these distractions are illusory, this constitutes the practice of this samadhi, and all the distractions are in fact friends of and enhancements to the meditation rather than hindrances or obstacles.

JAMGÖN KONGTRÜL LODRÖ THAYE (1813–1899)   A great Tibetan master, renowned for his scholarship and prolific work of compiling and composing texts.

KAGYU LINEAGE   "The lineage of the teachings." One of the four major Tibetan Buddhist lineages (the others being Nyingma, Sakya, and Geluk), it originated with the Buddha Vajradhara (symbolizing the Dharmakaya) to Tilopa, then Naropa, Marpa, Milarepa, and Gampopa. At that point, the lineage divided into many branches. The Karma Kagyu branch began with Gampopa's student Dusum Khyenpa, the First Karmapa. Today, Ogyen Trinley Dorje is the Seventeenth Karmapa.

KARMA/KARMIC ACTIONS   *Karma* literally means "action," but it can also refer to the results of actions as well. The actions that ordinary sentient beings take with body, speech, and mind, motivated by one or more kleshas and that result in suffering, are known as karmic actions.

KHENPO   A title conferred upon a Tibetan Buddhist teacher that indicates mastery of scholarship.

KLESHAS   The disturbing emotions and mental states that cause ordinary sentient beings to suffer as a result of their not having realized the true nature of reality. The five main kleshas, also called the "five poisons," are: attachment or desire; aversion or anger; stupidity or mental dullness; pride; and jealousy.

LOGICAL REASONING   A logical reasoning consists of: a subject about which an assertion is made; a quality that is asserted or denied with regard to that subject; and a reason that proves the subject has or does not have that quality. For example, in the logical reasoning "Suffering does not truly exist because it has no temporal duration," then "suffering" is the subject, "true existence" is the quality that suffering is denied possessing, and "because it has no temporal duration" is the reason why that is the case, for when one examines even the tiniest moment of time, one finds that it is divisible into an infinite number of smaller moments, and therefore no truly existent moment of time can be found.

LUMINOSITY-EMPTINESS   A way to describe mind's true nature as the union of the luminosity emphasized by the Empty-of-Other School and the emptiness taught in the Empty-of-Self school. For more explanation, see pages 112–14.

MAHAMUDRA   "Great seal." A profound set of instructions that describe the true nature of reality as clarity-emptiness or bliss-emptiness, and explain how to meditate upon this true nature.

MAHAYANA   The "great vehicle" of Buddhism, it is the path of practicing the two types of bodhichitta; of wisdom and compassion together. Practitioners begin Mahayana practice by engendering love, compassion, and relative bodhichitta, and then train in the six transcendent practices (Skt.: *paramitas*): generosity, ethics, patience, joyous diligence, concentration, and ultimate bodhichitta—the wisdom that realizes the true nature of reality—with the goal of attaining the enlightenment of the buddhas in order to lead all sentient beings to that same state.

MAITREYA   Of all the noble bodhisattvas, Maitreya is the Buddha Shakyamuni's regent and will be the next buddha. He is the author of the *Five Treatises of Maitreya*: *Distinguishing the Middle and the Extremes, Distinguishing Phenomena and Their Essential Reality, The Ornament of the Mahayana Sutras, The Ornament of Direct Realization,* and *The Treatise on Buddha Nature.*

MANJUSHRI   The noble bodhisattva and yidam deity who is taught to be the embodiment of all the buddhas' wisdom.

MARPA THE TRANSLATOR (1012–1097)   A great Tibetan master and one of the founders of the Kagyu lineage. When Marpa was young, he had a ferocious temper and was known as a bully. His parents worried that he would either kill another person or be killed himself, so they arranged for him to learn and practice the Dharma. Marpa made three arduous journeys to India and brought many teachings back with him to Tibet, which he translated into Tibetan in order to benefit the people of his native land. He became the teacher of Milarepa.

MIDDLE WAY SCHOOLS (Skt.: *Madhyamaka*)   The philosophical tenets that explain the emptiness of phenomena in a profound way, the Empty-of-Self and Empty-of-Other schools. The former is divided into the Autonomy and Consequence schools.

MILAREPA (1040–1123)   A student of Marpa the Translator, this great yogi attained the state of buddhahood in a single lifetime and was one of the founders of the Kagyu lineage of Tibetan Buddhism. He is revered for having overcome suffering and having persevered through hardship and austerity on his triumphant journey to enlightenment. His songs about his experiences and realization are renowned.

MIND-ONLY SCHOOL (Skt.: *Chittamatra*)   A Mahayana philosophical school. Its view is that outer objects do not truly exist; instead, they are the confused projections of mind's habitual tendencies, like appearances in dreams. Since outer objects of perception do not truly exist, neither do their perceiving subjects, and so genuine reality is empty of the duality of perceived and perceiver. Genuine reality is nondual consciousness, mere lucid awareness.

MIND TRAINING   A system of training in bodhichitta, both ulti-mate and relative. *The Seven Points of Mind Training* is a famous text that teaches this system.

MODE OF APPEARANCE   The way that any particular phenome-non appears to be. For confused sentient beings, phenomena appear to be truly existent. Synonymous with "relative reality."

MODE OF UNDERLYING REALITY   An appearance's true nature, which includes the qualities of impermanence and emptiness of true existence. Synonymous with "genuine reality."

NAGARJUNA   Indian master, born four hundred years after the Buddha's passing (ca. 544 B.C.E.). He is the author of *The Fundamen-tal Wisdom of the Middle Way* and other commentaries on the Bud-dha's teachings in all three turnings of the wheel of Dharma.

NAROPA (eleventh century)   A famous scholar at Nalanda Univer-sity in India, Naropa left his academic post when he realized that al-though he was a master of the Dharma's words, he had not fully internalized their meaning. On the banks of a river he met his teacher Tilopa, who was living as an outcaste, and he went on to endure the many difficult trials that Tilopa put him through before pointing out to him the true nature of his mind. At that point, Naropa realized the true meaning of Dharma and became a great siddha. He was the teacher of Marpa the Translator.

NIRVANA   "Transcendence of suffering," the liberation from sam-sara that is achieved, according to the vehicle of the hearers and the vehicle of the solitary realizers, when one realizes the selflessness of the individual sentient being. According to the Mahayana, the only authentic nirvana is the state of buddhahood, which, due to the per-fection of the wisdom that realizes the emptiness of all phenomena, does not fall into the extreme of samsaric existence and, due to the perfection of compassion, does not fall into the extreme of peace (as the nirvana achieved by the arhats does).

PADMASAMBHAVA   Also known as Guru Rinpoche, one of the original Dzogchen masters, a founder of the Nyingma lineage, and a key figure in the early propagation of Dharma in Tibet in the eighth century.

PALTRUL RINPOCHE (1808–1887)   A famous scholar and meditation master, and author of *Words of My Perfect Teacher,* a classic text on the stages of Buddhist practice, and *A Discourse Virtuous in the Beginning, Middle, and End,* a text that combines profound teachings on the view of genuine reality with meditation on Chenrezik, the noble bodhisattva and yidam deity who is the embodiment of compassion.

PROTECTORS   The protectors are Vajrayana deities who protect the teachings of Dharma from those who may wish to do them harm, and who clear away obstacles from the path of the practitioner. The most important and effective protector is taught to be one's own realization of emptiness and equality, which turns enemies into friends and obstacles into enhancements of one's practice.

RAINBOW BODY   The rainbow body is achieved by advanced practitioners who realize the nonduality of matter and mind. Such practitioners can dissolve their bodies into rainbow light and emanate physical appearance again in the same or different realms. It is similar to the ability one has to transform and emanate one's body in a lucid dream.

RELATIVE REALITY   The realm of all material and mental appearances, which confused sentient beings believe to be truly existent, as when one dreams and does not know that one is dreaming.

RENUNCIATION   To abandon searching for happiness in the dualistic appearances of samsara.

RINPOCHE   "Precious one." A Tibetan title of highest esteem that Buddhist students use to address their teacher.

SAMADHI   Meditation; any meditative state of concentration. Literally defined as "holding the mind one-pointedly on its object of focus."

Samsara   The "cycle" of existence in which sentient beings who do not realize the true nature of reality wander from one lifetime to the next, experiencing constant suffering. More subtly, whenever one believes that oneself and the dualistic appearances of object and subject truly exist, one is vulnerable to disturbing emotions and suffering, and so one is in samsara.

Saraha   A great Indian master of Vajrayana and Mahamudra, and the teacher of Nagarjuna.

Self-awareness   Nondual, inexpressible awareness that both the Mind-Only and Empty-of-Other schools assert is the true nature of mind. The Mind-Only school asserts self-awareness to be a truly existent entity; whereas the Empty-of-Other school asserts that self-awareness is not a truly existent entity, it is luminosity-emptiness inseparable.

Selflessness of the individual   When sentient beings believe the self—the object referred to by thoughts of "I" and "me"—to be truly existent, that is a confused belief that is the source of all suffering. However, in genuine reality, the self does not exist. Therefore, the "I" and "me" that appear in relative reality are dependently arisen mere appearances. This view of selflessness is held in common by all Buddhist philosophical schools. See also Aggregates.

Self-liberation   Primarily, the freedom that is an inherent quality of the true nature of appearances and mind. Since appearances are by nature appearance-emptiness, and thoughts and emotions are by nature clarity-emptiness, they need no outside liberator to set them free. Just as when one is bound by iron chains in a dream, the perfect remedy is to realize that one is dreaming, so one must only realize the true nature of one's experiences to gain liberation from whatever difficulties they may present.

In the Mahamudra and Dzogchen traditions, phenomena are described as self-liberated for the above reason and also because they are "self-arisen," meaning that they have no truly existent causes for their arising.

Shamatha "Calm-abiding" meditation, which occurs when mind's distracted movements calm down, and mind abides one-pointedly on the meditation's object of focus.

Shantarakshita (eighth century)   Great Indian proponent of the Middle Way Autonomy school and author of *Ornament of the Middle Way*.

Shantideva (seventh to eighth century)   Great Indian master and author of *Entering the Bodhisattvas' Way*, a famous compendium of Mahayana practice and the view of the Middle Way Consequence school.

Siddha   "One who has gained siddhi." A practitioner who has realized the true nature of reality.

Siddhi   "Accomplishment of one's meditative practice." There are two kinds of siddhis, common and supreme. The common siddhis refer to various kinds of special mental and physical powers that one can realize via a variety of Buddhist and non-Buddhist meditative practices. Far more important is the supreme siddhi, the direct realization of the true nature of mind and all its qualities of emptiness, compassion, clarity, and great bliss.

Six realms   The six classes of sentient beings, divided into three higher realms: gods, demigods, and humans; and three lower realms: animals, hungry ghosts, and hell beings. These six realms constitute samsara; and sentient beings, depending on their mix of previous positive and negative attitudes and actions that constitute their karma, wander from rebirth in one realm to rebirth in either that same realm or others, until they gain liberation by realizing the true nature of reality.

Sutra   In Buddhism, a discourse given by the Buddha at a particular time and place. Furthermore, when the Buddha specifically instructed one of his disciples to give a discourse, and when the discourse was given by a disciple through the power of the Buddha's blessing (as with *The Heart Sutra*), those teachings were also classified as the Buddha's own sutras.

TARA   A female noble bodhisattva and yidam deity who is renowned for her abilities to protect sentient beings from fear and to
help them accomplish their aims in harmony with the Dharma. She
is also known as the "Noble Liberator."

THREE KAYAS   The three dimensions of enlightenment; in the
Mahamudra and Dzogchen teachings, the three dimensions of the
true nature of mind. In the former explanation, the Dharmakaya is a
buddha's enlightened mind; Sambhogakaya is the subtle-light form
in which a buddha appears to noble bodhisattvas; and Nirmanakaya
is the material body in which a buddha appears to noble bodhisattvas and ordinary sentient beings alike.

   In the explanation connecting the three kayas with the true nature
of mind, Dharmakaya is mind's emptiness of essence; Sambhogakaya
is mind's natural clarity and luminosity; and Nirmanakaya is mind's
ability to appear as and cognize an unimpeded variety of images.

THREE REALMS   The desire, form, and formless realms are home
to all sentient beings in samsara. Most sentient beings, including
animals and humans, inhabit the desire realm, so named because desire for physical and mental pleasure and happiness is the overriding
mental experience of beings in this realm. The form and formless
realms are populated by gods in various meditative states who are
very attached to meditative experiences of clarity and the total absence of thoughts, respectively.

THREE TURNINGS OF THE WHEEL OF DHARMA   The three sets
of teachings that the Buddha gave. In the first turning, the Buddha
taught that samsara is of the nature of suffering and that one can
attain nirvana by practicing the Dharma. In the second turning, the
Buddha taught that everything in samsara and nirvana is of the
nature of emptiness. In the third turning, the Buddha taught about
the buddha nature, the enlightened essence of luminous clarity that
is the true nature of the mind of every sentient being.

TILOPA (tenth to eleventh century)   A great Indian master who
abandoned life as a prince (some sources say Brahman priest) to seek

realization on the path of Dharma. However, he did not gain realization until he learned how to meditate while working at ordinary jobs—crushing sesame seeds by day, and working at a beerhouse by night. He became the main teacher of Naropa.

TONGLEN   "Sending and taking," a *Mind Training* practice of love and compassion that one connects with one's breathing. When one exhales, one sends out all of one's happiness and virtue to others; when one inhales, one takes into oneself all of their suffering and negativity in the form of dark smoke, and purifies them in one's heart, which one imagines to be a bright sphere of pure light, inseparable from emptiness.

TRANSCENDENT WISDOM SUTRAS (Skt.: *Prajnaparamita Sutras*) The sutras that constitute the second turning of the wheel of Dharma and teach that all phenomena's true nature is emptiness, beyond conceptual fabrication, and perfect purity. By training in this, one develops transcendent wisdom, and when one perfects this wisdom, one attains the enlightenment of the buddhas.

TREATISE ON BUDDHA NATURE (Tib.: *Gyu Lama*; Skt.: *Uttaratantrashastra*)   Composed by the bodhisattva Maitreya, this text explains how and why the true nature of every sentient being's mind is the buddha nature, original wisdom, the pure essence of enlightenment. It also describes the buddhas' enlightenment, enlightenment's qualities, and the buddhas' enlightened activities. The text is based on the Buddha's teachings in the third turning of the wheel of Dharma. See Buddha nature.

TRULKHOR   Generally, the physical yogic exercises taught in the Vajrayana. However, Milarepa explains that when one rests one's mind in its own basic nature and moves one's body, all of one's physical movements are trulkhor.

TWO TRUTHS   The Buddha taught that if we analyze, we come to see that the way things appear to be are not the way they truly are. So he taught the truth of relative reality, which is how things appear to be, and the truth of genuine reality, phenomena's true nature. Ultimately, he taught that the two truths are inseparable, beyond the conceptual fabrications of "same" and "different." See Genuine reality and Relative reality.

VAJRA "Adamantine." A synonym for the indestructible buddha nature that is the true nature of the mind.

VAJRAYANA "Adamantine vehicle." It is the set of Mahayana practices that one learns in stages under the supervision of a qualified teacher, and that practitioners keep secret from those who have not been initiated into the same levels of practice.

VEHICLE (Skt.: *yana*) A section of the Buddha's teachings that contains a complete set of instructions on view, meditation, and conduct necessary to reach a particular level of realization. The name derives from the metaphor of using these teachings to carry us on the journey to the fruition of a particular path. There are different presentations of how many yanas there are—sometimes three, sometimes nine; once the Buddha even taught that there is a different yana for each different concept we have, because each concept contains an element of confusion that we need to know how to transcend.

VEHICLE OF THE HEARERS (Skt.: *Shravaka-yana*) One of two vehicles whose practices are based on the Buddha's teachings in the first turning of the wheel of Dharma. Its name is derived from the quality of how intently its followers listen to the Buddha's teachings. The fruition of this vehicle is the attainment of the level of arhat.

VEHICLE OF THE SOLITARY REALIZERS (Skt.: *Pratekya-buddha-yana*) One of two vehicles whose practices are based on the Buddha's teachings in the first turning of the wheel of Dharma. As a result of pride, followers of this path desire to attain realization by themselves, without a teacher or other students around. Thus, in their final lifetime as an ordinary sentient being, they are born in a place where the Buddhist teachings do not otherwise exist. Due to a certain set of circumstances, their past knowledge and habits awaken, and they are able to attain the state of arhat all by themselves, hence their name.

VIPASHYANA   "Superior insight" meditation, which occurs when there is insight in meditation into the superior object of the true nature of reality.

YIDAM   A deity whom one supplicates and meditates upon in Vajrayana practice. Khenpo Tsültrim Gyamtso Rinpoche emphasizes that like all phenomena, these deities are not truly existent, and their genuine nature is inseparable from the buddha nature, the true nature of mind.

YOGA   "To join with naturalness." Any practice that helps its practitioners to realize the true nature of reality.

YOGI/YOGINI   Male (yogi) and female (yogini) practitioners who have "joined with naturalness," meaning that they have realized the true nature of reality to one degree or another. Thus, there are hearer-yogis, solitary-realizer-yogis, bodhisattva-yogis, and buddha-yogis, the last of these being the most advanced yogis of all. Practitioners on the paths to these fruitions can also be called yogis and yoginis.

Sources of the Teachings

Chapter 1, "The Path of Faith and the Path of Reasoning," comes from a teaching by Khenpo Tsültrim Gyamtso Rinpoche at Karma Thegsum Choling, Palo Alto, California, on June 7, 1997.

Chapter 2, "The Stages of View at the Heart of Definitive Meaning," contains a text in verse of the same name that Khenpo Rinpoche composed in various places in the United States and in Kathmandu, Nepal, in 1993–1994. With Rinpoche's permission, the translators have added verses on meditation that he composed in Brussels, Belgium, in 2003. This chapter also contains his explanations of the meaning of this text and his answers to students' questions about it from teaching sessions in Kathmandu, in 1994.

Chapter 4, "The Seven Ways Things Shine Inside and Out," comes from the explanations of Milarepa's song of the same name and responses to students' questions that Khenpo Rinpoche gave at Pullahari Monastery, Kathmandu, Nepal, in January 2000; Wellington Shambhala Center, Wellington, New Zealand, in October 2000; and Kagyu Thegsum Choling, Shamong, New Jersey, in October 2005.

Chapter 5, "The Eighteen Kinds of Yogic Joy," comes from Khenpo Rinpoche's explanations of Milarepa's song of the same name and responses to students' questions about it given at the Rigpe Dorje Retreat in San Antonio, Texas, in September 1999; at Boulder Shambhala Center, Boulder, Colorado, in November 2005; and at Kagyu Thegchen Ling, Honolulu, Hawaii, in January 2006.

Resources

PLEASE VISIT www.starsofwisdom.info to find the Tibetan texts and songs that are explained in this book, audio files of the melodies for the English translations of the songs, *Stars of Wisdom* teaching schedule information, and more.

Please visit www.ktgrinpoche.org for information on Khenpo Tsültrim Gyamtso Rinpoche and Marpa Foundation's Dharma activities.

Index

abiding nature, 52, 112–13. *See also* Dharmata; reality, genuine; reality, true nature of; true nature

aggregates, 23–31, 32

alaya-vijnana. See base consciousness

all-base consciousness. *See* base consciousness

altruism, 32–33; benefits of, 107, 116; karma and, 80; wisdom and, 135. *See also* compassion; love; lovingkindness

Amka Sembewa, 121

analysis, 3–6; of appearance, 6–8, 10–15; of body, 14, 23–24; of fear, 117–18; of five aggregates, 23–31; of genuine reality, 61; importance of, 12–13, 14; of mind, 112–13, 128; in Mind-Only school, 38; when suffering, 16–17

anger, 51, 87, 121

animals, 109, 124

apparent reality. *See* reality, relative

appearance, 65–66, 92, 97, 111; analyzing, 5, 6–8, 10–15; in Empty-of-Self tradition, 47–48, 49–52; Mind-Only view of, 33–36, 46; in realms of existence, 42–43, 44–45, 89–90; variety of, 114–16

appearance-emptiness, 45, 56, 93, 125; of environment, 111–12; in Mind-Only school, 36; of phenomena, 97; rainbow analogy, 110; of the self, 22; of the three realms, 90

Aryadeva, 95–96

aspiration prayers, 133–37, 139–41, 143–46

assertions, 55

attributes, 49

Autonomy school, 55–56, 64

Avatamsaka Sutra, The, 105

bardo, 79

base-consciousness, 79–80

beings, sentient, 58; aspiration prayer for,

139–41; compassion for, 61–62, 86; perceptions of, 33–34, 35

birth, 134; as appearance, 51–52, 119; of bodhisattvas, 62. *See also* human life, precious

bliss, 58, 76, 113–14, 123, 126–27, 128–29

bodhichitta, 62–63, 88, 101–2, 146

bodhisattvas, 51, 58, 63, 66, 137; activity of, 61–62; realization of, 100

body: analysis of, 14, 23–24; Mind-Only view of, 34–36; natural yoga of, 123. *See also* human life, precious

bondage, 52–53, 90

buddhahood, 62

buddha nature, 57–59, 97, 134

buddhas, 58, 66, 95, 137

Buddha Shakyamuni, 21, 36; on analysis, 4; compassion of, 136; speech of, 71, 73

Buddhism: dance traditions in, 123; language and culture of, 73–74; selflessness in, 32; singing tradition of, 71–72; vehicles of, 12, 62. *See also* Dharma

causes and conditions, 8; for Dharma songs, 124; in Empty-of-Self tradition, 47–48; impermanence and, 94–95

certainty, 4, 17–19, 42–43, 50; compassion and, 87–88; in equal taste, 99–100; in Middle Way school, 55–56, 60; in Mind-Only school, 46; resting in, 117, 122; in selflessness, 31–32; about wisdom, 91

chakras, 72–73

channels, 72–73

characteristics, 26, 39

charnel grounds, 118, 120

Chittamatra. *See* Mind-Only school

Chö, 118, 120

clarity, luminous, 57, 97, 113, 128

clarity-emptiness. *See* luminosity-emptiness

clinging, 51–52, 85, 144; to aggregates, 24,

About the Author

KHENPO TSÜLTRIM GYAMTSO RINPOCHE is a Buddhist master, renowned for possessing the intellect and knowledge of a scholar and the realization, humor, and creativity of a yogi. He is a teacher of H. H. the Seventeenth Gyalwang Karmapa and other high-ranking lamas of the Kagyu lineage. Yet people all over the world appreciate him for his willingness to share the most profound teachings of Buddhism with lamas and laypeople, women and men, and practitioners old and new alike.

Khenpo Rinpoche was born in 1934 to a nomad family in Eastern Tibet. When he was two years old, his father died suddenly. Thereafter, his mother devoted herself full-time to Dharma practice. As her youngest child, Rinpoche accompanied her on pilgrimages and to Dharma teachings, even staying by her side when she undertook extended retreats. By nature and nurture drawn to spiritual practice, Rinpoche left home at an early age to train with yogis who lived and practiced in the remote monasteries and caves of Eastern and Central Tibet.

After completing this early training, Rinpoche embraced the life of a yogi-ascetic. For years he wandered throughout Eastern and Central Tibet, undertaking solitary retreats in caves and charnel grounds to realize directly the teachings he had received.

While in such a retreat in 1959, a group of twenty-one nuns asked Rinpoche for protection from the Communist Chinese invaders.

When they told him that H. H. the Fourteenth Dalai Lama and H. H. the Sixteenth Gyalwang Karmapa had already left Tibet, Rinpoche replied, "Then we are going, too!" Rinpoche led the nuns and other refugees over the Himalayas to safety in Bhutan.

Rinpoche spent the next nine years at a scholastic monastery for Tibetan refugees on the grounds of an old prison yard in Buxa Duar, India. There he studied intensively, mastering the teachings of all four schools of Tibetan Buddhism. He became renowned as a teacher of texts and meditation, and received a Geshe Lharampa degree from H. H. the Fourteenth Dalai Lama. He lived, practiced, and taught in Bhutan from 1968 until 1977.

At the request of H. H. the Sixteenth Gyalwang Karmapa, in 1977 Rinpoche began teaching Dharma and classical Tibetan Dharma language abroad. For thirty years, Rinpoche traveled and taught extensively in Europe, North America, South America, Asia, Africa, and Australia. Rinpoche was a pioneer in giving careful, long-term training to Buddhist translators. During this time, Rinpoche also spent several months a year training a new generation of Kagyu khenpos at the Karmapa's Nalanda Institute in Sikkim, India.

Rinpoche is committed to providing nuns with the same opportunities for study and practice that monks traditionally have. To that end, he established one nunnery in Nepal and one in Bhutan. The women at these nunneries study and practice the profound view and meditation, and sing and dance to the profound songs of realization.

For the years Rinpoche spent teaching worldwide, when asked, "Where do you live?" he usually replied, "On the planet Earth." At this time in his life, however, Rinpoche has retired from traveling and teaching publicly, and spends his time between his nunneries in Bhutan and Nepal.

About the Translators

ARI GOLDFIELD is a Buddhist translator and teacher who has studied and practiced under the close guidance of Khenpo Tsültrim Gyamtso Rinpoche since 1995. He has translated books, articles, and numerous songs of realization and texts on Buddhist philosophy and meditation, including Khenpo Rinpoche's *Song of the Eight Flashing Lances* teaching, which appeared in *The Best Buddhist Writing* 2007, Khenpo Rinpoche's book *The Sun of Wisdom,* and *The Moon of Wisdom.* He studied Buddhist texts in Tibetan and Sanskrit at Buddhist monasteries in Nepal and India, and at the Central Institute for Higher Tibetan Studies in India. From 1998 to 2006 he served as Khenpo Rinpoche's full-time secretary and translator on seven round-the-world teaching tours. He has also served as translator for H. H. the Seventeenth Gyalwang Karmapa, Tenga Rinpoche, and many other Tibetan teachers. In 2006, Khenpo Rinpoche stayed in retreat and sent Ari on his own tour to teach philosophy, meditation, and yogic exercise in Europe, North America, and Asia. In 2007, Khenpo Rinpoche appointed him president of the Marpa Foundation, a nonprofit organization that supports nunneries in Bhutan and Nepal, Buddhist translation, and other Buddhist activities. Ari holds a BA from Harvard College and a JD from Harvard Law School, both with honors.

ROSE TAYLOR is a Buddhist translator and second-generation Buddhist teacher. She teaches Buddhist meditation, philosophy, yogic exercise and dance, and classical Tibetan language to Westerners, as well as to the nuns at Khenpo Tsültrim Gyamtso Rinpoche's nunneries in Bhutan and Nepal. She holds an MA in Indo-Tibetan Buddhist studies from Naropa University. Having studied and practiced extensively in the Shambhala lineage, in which her mother is also a longtime student and teacher, she began training under Khenpo Rinpoche's close guidance in 2002. In 2007, Khenpo Rinpoche appointed her vice president and secretary of Marpa Foundation.

Rose and Ari currently work for Marpa Foundation, translate, and teach internationally from their home base in the San Francisco Bay Area.

ALSO BY KHENPO TSÜLTRIM GYAMTSO

The Sun of Wisdom: Teachings on the Noble Nagarjuna's
Fundamental Wisdom of the Middle Way

The Fundamental Wisdom of the Middle Way was written in the second century and is one of the most important works of Nagarjuna, the pioneering commentator on the Buddha's teachings on the Madhyamika or Middle Way view. The subtle analyses presented in this treatise were closely studied and commented upon by many realized masters from the Iado-Tibetan tradition.

Using Nagajuna's root text and the great modern master Ju Mipham's commentary as a framework, Khenpo Tsültrim Gyamtso Rinpoche explains the text in a style that illuminates for modern students both the meaning of these profound teachings and how to put them into practice in a way that benefits both oneself and others.